MW00721065

Where Mountains Touch Heaven

Eva Kingsnorth Powell

Where Mountains Touch Heaven

Ena Kingsnorth Powell

hancock

house

ISBN 0-88839-365-2

Cataloging in Publication Data
Powell, Ena Kingsnorth, 1925-
   Where mountains touch heaven
   ISBN 0-88839-365-2

   I. Title.
PS8581.093W53 1995 C813'.54 C95-910633-2
PR9199.3.P68W53 1995

Editor: Colin Lamont
Cover Design: Karen Whitman
Production: Myron Shutty and Nancy Kerr

Published simultaneously in Canada and the United States by

HANCOCK HOUSE PUBLISHERS LTD.
19313 Zero Avenue, Surrey, B.C. V4P 1M7
(604) 538-1114 Fax (604) 538-2262

HANCOCK HOUSE PUBLISHERS
1431 Harrison Avenue, Blaine, WA 98230-5005
(604) 538-1114 Fax (604) 538-2262

Contents

Prologue

A Rocky Mountain bighorn sheep staggered over the field and hid behind the barn when he saw the man. The man went to investigate, and was confronted by a massive set of horns and watchful eyes. There was a large gash across the ram's chest, he sank to the ground and lay in the spring sun; the blood from his wound soaked the earth. The man was reminded of his wife's blood flowing forth at the birth of their son, nearly ending her life, on that very day. He went into the barn and brought water and oats for the suffering animal. When the mother and baby came home from the hospital the sheep was standing by the corral, watching. This happened in Golden, British Columbia, on May 1, 1975.

Introduction

Each year before winter shrouds the earth with snow in the Interior Valley of British Columbia, there is a short period of splendor called Indian summer. According to a legend, "The Indians' war paint has rubbed off on the leaves and colored them red." The sky turns a rich blue and the warm autumn days are followed by chilly nights. A haze appears on the horizon and the moon has an orange hue. When God's gift ends, winter begins. At this time the bighorn sheep follow their instinct to the mating season.

The ram with its astrological associations, (the first sign in the zodiac) has piqued the love of mystery, the desire to foretell events in the universe, and the fortunes of the lives of man and womankind for thousands of years, and continues to do so. Our story begins with one ram in particular, who chose to live his life on the western slope of the Canadian Rockies, close to civilization.

You reach this ram's lofty home after leaving the Rogers Pass in the Selkirk Mountains, and before going through the Rockies to Lake Louise and Banff. It's called the Columbia Valley, where the Kicking Horse River joins the Columbia River on its long journey through Washington and Oregon to the sea. In the valley where the two rivers meet is the town of Golden, where it has reposed since the first trading post was established. Golden was first called Golden City to "go one better," after a rival settlement called Carlin's Camp changed its name to Silver City. Golden City later became, and remains, Golden.

While the Selkirks on the west and the Rockies on the east rise in competition for the merit of contributing the most beauty to the valley, the Kicking Horse River runs through town to join the Columbia and steal the show. The Kicking Horse was named when a geologist, Dr. James Hector, with the Palliser expedition, sent to locate a feasible route for the Canadian Pacific Railroad through the mountains, was kicked in the chest by his own horse while camped near the Great Divide.

About half a mile from town on the west side is Edelweiss, a replica of a little Swiss village. It was constructed by the C.P.R. before the First World War to house the Swiss guides brought from Switzerland to assist tourists using the Canadian Pacific Hotels in the area, so that the beauty of the surrounding mountains could be safely enjoyed. On the east side of town where the mountains rise and the Trans Canada Highway winds its way upwards to the Kicking Horse Pass, there is a spread of bench land that looks over the entire valley.

On this bench where many pioneers took up homesteads around the turn of the century, and just before the mountain itself rises again to its ultimate height, is Windsong. The rolling acres that comprise this ranch are rich in timber as well as grass for grazing.

Only the roof of the ranch house can be seen when you come in through the gate, but the yard is level and spacious. On one side is a cluster of barns and sheds with an attached corral and a haystack enclosed by a barbed wire fence. A clearing above the yard rises gradually to where the land becomes too steep for practical use and the bush begins. Beyond the barn is a small ravine where a creek runs down to fill the pond in the meadow below. The low rambling house nestles against the bank before the land drops off to the meadow and the pond, and commands a sweeping view of the mountains and valley.

The yard is dotted with pine, fir, and cedar trees that scent the air, as well as poplar, whose summer host of leaves affords welcome respite from the heat of the day and adds a rhythmic tinkling sound to the song the trees sing when the wind blows down from the spiraling peaks above.

The barns show spots of red where paint was once applied and then left to weather, now brown with stain along with the adjoining sheds, from the wind and the rain and the sun in the changing seasons. The meadow hosts an abundance of green grass in the spring and summer that turns brown in the fall in readiness for winter, when icy wind blows from the Rockies and the animals paw through the snow to retrieve the welcome feed. Rushes grow in the pond and the brown cattails can be picked in the fall and dipped for dry floral arrangements if caught before they burst, leaving the scattering of their seeds to the discretion of the wind. When the temperature drops, ice forms, and the pond becomes a wonderful place for skating, providing one's enthusiasm keeps pace with removing the four or five feet of snow that falls, turning Windsong into a special winterland of beauty.

When a full moon beams through the still cold air and dances on the glistening snow, the children playing hockey have no need for the light from the roaring bonfire.

A rocky bluff rises above the meadow by the pond, where the house with its many windows to the west reposes in an aura of warmth and welcome. The highway and town are hidden by trees. The silver river winds through the valley, while the mountains rise from dense forests to pinnacles of lofty measure.

This gives the beholder the feeling that this place is still molded in its original cast, while over the decades of its existence, evolution was forever present. An evolution that is displayed in everything from the lichen on the rocks, to the hoodoos, to the ever-changing face of the mountains themselves in their moods of light and shadow. And so the majesty of Windsong on the western slope of the Rockies is carried on from mountain to mountain, to Banff, and to the Alberta plains, where their beauty can still be seen and enjoyed. It was this feeling of majesty and power that filled the heart of Cyrus Logan when he first glimpsed the Rockies from the window of the train on his way west. After finishing engineering studies at

McGill University in Montreal, he was engaged by the C.P.R. to construct the Spiral Tunnels near Field, B.C.

Believing as he did that, "as the twig is bent so the branch shall grow," something deep within him stirred, filling him with dreams. He wondered to what heights sons and daughters born and raised in these magnificent surroundings could aspire. Would some of the strength and power that was here, where the spectre of the brocken occurs (an optical illusion visible when the sun is low, casting seemingly gigantic silhouettes from mountain peaks on low-lying clouds) inspire his children and their descendants? He believed that it would.

This giant of a man with a will of iron and nerves of steel decided then and there he would one day own a mountain.

On his first visit to Golden he met and fell in love with Effie Russell. When they were married he purchased the highest tract of land on the mountain that could be found. So happy were they at their retreat, lulled by the sound of the wind singing in the trees, that they called it Windsong.

In those days, access to the ranch was so long and difficult they used Windsong only as a retreat when Cyrus was home. His reputation as an engineer took him far and wide after he finished the Spiral Tunnels, the engineering feat of the century. He became famous for his brilliance in the field of engineering and for his ability to handle other men.

Cyrus and Effie lived in town where she bore him three fine sons. A fourth child, a girl, died at birth and when there were to be no more children, their happiness was marred for a time. Life was hard and cruel, but coming as they did from hardy stock they survived, and took a great deal of pleasure in their sons.

During the Second World War, while all three sons were overseas, Cyrus and Effie lived in dread of losing them, but they were among the fortunate parents. Their boys returned; Gregory to a ranch in southern Alberta near Brooks; Norman joined an oil company in Calgary, and advanced to an executive position; and Russell, who was a distinguished flyer with the Royal Canadian Air Force, a "Flying Ace"—one of Canada's six—finished his studies in law at the University of British Columbia and set up his own law firm in Golden.

Russell was a very busy lawyer, and Cyrus, who had retired, spent many hours at Windsong with Brian, the grandson he adored. They rode in the mountains and fished in the streams. They camped out overnight, in summer and in winter, and sat on the deck of the cabin watching the sun set behind the Selkirk Mountains, a bond between them so intense that even in silence it was there. It was a bitter disappointment to Cyrus when the grandson he so dearly loved became a school teacher instead of the engineer his grandfather was determined that he would become. But the old man was overjoyed years later, at the birth of Brian and Joanne's baby son, Christopher Cyrus, a strong healthy boy to carry on the Logan heritage.

Cyrus and Effie lived a long and happy life until she passed away, leaving him to mourn for a short time before joining her in the little cemetery on the hill in Golden. The die was cast. This powerful man was to influence the lives of his descendants for years to come.

1   Father and Son

The horses were standing near the fence at the top of the pasture, and a dog was sleeping by the house in the sun. A Rocky Mountain bighorn sheep, the most beautiful wild animal known to man, stepped forward like a statesman in a senate, ever listening, ever watchful for any movement or sound, while placidly chewing his cud. His intelligent brown eyes matched the gray-brown of his coat on the upper part of his body that became darker brown underneath. The white of his nose matched the white pillow of his rump, broken only by the black line of his tail. His massive horns curled forward to a sharp point, and a raised spot on the back of his head between his horns where the hair grew straight up was a personal distinction suggesting a battle scar.

He was trying to drive the horses to some place other than where they were, contentedly watching the meadow below for any movement to break the still of the lazy afternoon. When the horses failed to heed his efforts, the sheep approached a post that was supporting the wires that formed the fence, and proceeded to punish it severely by ramming it with his horns. After tiring of this, he jumped the fence from a standing position and strolled past the house, stopping a minute to peer in a window, before continuing across the yard and entering the clearing above the ranch where he disappeared into the surrounding bush.

The horses watched the ram leave, and with as little expression as horses portray, almost showed their relief at his departure.

The dog hadn't bothered to do more than lazily open his eyes and close them again when the ram passed by. It was evident that the sheep's presence in their domain was, although an unnatural one, an accepted one. This bossy, overbearing wild animal was without right dominating the scene where the other animals belonged.

Very few mountain sheep inhabit this part of the Rockies, and the ones that do live in the remote wilderness areas where it is steep and rocky. This sheep roamed the ranch as if it belonged to him. His reason for being there was something of a mystery.

The mountains that tower above the town were already capped with snow as Christopher sat on the school swing idly dragging one foot as he pushed himself back and forth. A gentle breeze with the hint of fall tossed his blond curls over his face. The beauty of the surrounding country was lost to Christopher. It had seemed to him that the school day would never end, and as he sat on the swing, it seemed to him that his father would never come. He hadn't been able to concentrate on the teacher's lessons, and several times she had stopped to reprimand him, but he couldn't stop thinking about his mother. He missed her and wanted her to come back. Thinking of what to say to her had occupied him ever since he got the idea of having Sam, the wild sheep, take him to see her.

Chris, as his father called him—except when he was angry—was a big boy with large blue eyes, pink cheeks and a pointed chin, who carried himself with a maturity beyond his tender years. He was bright and interested during his first few days at school, but had become withdrawn and preoccupied of late. His shoulders stooped in concentration, and his head rested on the back of his neck making his pointed chin stick out. His jaws were clamped tightly together in determination. He freed a hand from the swing to brush the hair away from his eyes so he could continue to watch the road leading to the school. His jacket and lunch kit lay on the ground where he had dropped them.

As the last bell of the day rang out to clear the grounds, a pickup truck came into view around the corner and headed down the road towards the school. Christopher jumped off the swing, picked up his jacket and lunch kit, and ran to the road. The truck stopped and as Christopher reached for the door handle, the door was opened from inside.

Brian Logan's eyes were large and blue, the same as his son's; his hair had darkened as he grew older, but traces of the curls were still there. He was a big man, tall with broad shoulders, an angular face and square chin. His outdoor life showed in his weathered skin and muscular body. As he looked at his son, the anxiety that covered his countenance was replaced with a look of tenderness unusual in a man of his nature. "Hi Chris." He was glad to see the solemn face of his son break into a smile.

"Hi Dad." Chris climbed in and closed the door. The truck turned around and moved down the road to the main street of the town. It passed the Overwaitea store, McLeods, and Steadmans before the street curved left by the Golden Civic Centre, and a stand of mountain ash trees, red with clusters of plump little berries, came into view. A flock of birds, banded together for the flight south, were chattering noisily as they became intoxicated from the elegant fruit on which they were feeding.

Buildings, whose design spoke of a bygone era, lined the street across from the quaint little train station. Many dignitaries, including kings and queens, had alighted on its platform over the years to shake hands and say a few words, before boarding the train again and traveling on to points east or west. The truck crossed the bridge over the Kicking Horse River, followed the bend of the road to the Trans-Canada Highway and took the highway up the hill.

"Didn't you have anyone to play with?" Brian asked, feeling bad about Chris being all alone when he picked him up.

"Kevin had to go home early. They're going away for the weekend tonight." Chris was silent for a few minutes, then he asked, "Can't we go tonight, Dad?"

14

"You know we can't go tonight, Chris, we discussed it already."

"I don't see why just you and me can't go."

There it was again. The evening he and Chris were discussing plans for their trip into the mountains, Jennifer had come into the family room and announced that she wanted to go with them. Brian had warned her that it might be a rough trip for someone so inexperienced at riding, but she had insisted she could handle it. Brian was thrilled until he saw a look of disappointment on his son's face. After that, Chris tried at every opportunity to discourage Jennifer from making the trip. When Brian asked his reasons for not wanting Jennifer along, Chris had been evasive and refused to answer. Brian became concerned about the relationship between his new wife and son. "Christopher, that's enough. I've explained a dozen times." Brian sounded annoyed, so they rode in silence.

At the top of the hill the truck left the highway and went up a steep incline to the left, out of sight of the town where the burners from the two sawmills hurled smoke into the cloudless sky, and followed along a narrow winding gravel road that went up and down for a while. There were roads leading off into the bush, but no houses could be seen. They turned off suddenly onto a dirt road that was barely visible and entered deep bush, where the shadows were long and slanted in the few places that the light was able to penetrate.

While maneuvering the truck along the narrow winding road, Brian was thinking about the problems of teaching in the community where he had grown up, when he realized that Chris had spoken.

"You what?"

"I told Kevin about Sam, but he didn't believe me."

"Chris, you know we keep Sam a secret so he will be safe. Why did you tell Kevin?" There was no answer, so he said, "Chris," then looking sideways he saw that Chris was sticking out his chin, his lips were pressed tightly together, and his eyes were staring straight ahead. Brian had an uneasy feeling about his son that worried him, as he looked at that tight little face, he knew from past experience that to pursue the questioning would be futile and would probably end by the loss of his own temper, so he drove the truck on through the bush in silence.

The trees were thinning out, and they were back in sunshine as they came to a gateway with a big rustic wooden sign that swung from poles standing on either side of the road that said, "Windsong" in big bold letters that had been burned into the wood, and underneath in smaller print, "The Logans." They passed under the sign and entered a clearing with a panoramic view of the valley and the surrounding mountains. The road leading to the ranch had such a gradual incline that it was surprising how high they were above the rest of the valley. They passed the barns and sheds with the attached corral where the horses were standing and moved on to the low house that stood on the edge of the bluff overlooking the meadow and pond.

Brian stopped the truck in front of the house and they got out. As Brian came around the truck he said, "Sam's not here."

"But he was here this morning when we left for school." Chris sounded surprised and a bit concerned.

"Maybe he just went out a ways to look things over, and then he'll come back." Brian started walking towards the house and Chris followed saying, "Maybe he's gone already and we should go right now to follow him."

"We can't go right now."

"But he will get away and we'll never find him."

"Tracks are easy to find in the soft earth in the bush, you know that."

"It might rain and wash the tracks away." He looked up at the cloudless blue sky as if wishing for a cloud to appear at which he could point, to further the threat.

"Christopher, there is no proof that Sam has gone for a lengthy stay. He may just have gone up in the bush like he does sometimes and come back again. If he is not back by morning, we will consider going after him. Now leave it at that." Brian hastened his steps towards the house. He knew that irritation had entered his voice and it bothered him. He had felt bad about being late to pick Chris up but had been detained at school because he had to speak with the parents of one of his basketball players. He loved his son dearly and felt a deep bond between them. They had been very close once, so close that Joanne, Brian's first wife and Christopher's real mother, had complained that she was left out, and had even shed tears over it. Lately, Brian thought that Chris had withdrawn and Brian couldn't get near him. He had been trying for weeks now to break the barrier between them and had got nowhere. That is why he had agreed to go along with his child's idea of following the ram.

He was trying to remember when the trouble had started with Chris. He and Jennifer were married, after Joanne's tragic death. He had worried about leaving Chris while they went on their honeymoon after the school had closed down in June. But Chris had seemed perfectly happy when they returned, and the three of them settled down at Windsong for the long lazy summer. They had barbecues on the patio, picnics by the pond in the meadow, and long hikes around Windsong and the adjoining trails. Sometime after that, Chris changed towards his "new Mom," as he referred to her, and Brian couldn't understand why.

As they continued towards the house, a dog bounded around the corner, panting after his long run up the hill from the pasture, having seen the truck come into the yard. He was a big German shepherd and collie cross, with the shepherd coloring and the collie size and coat, heavy in the chest with strong legs and big feet. He had the collie instinct to herd and the shepherd instinct to protect. Brian brought him home from Vancouver when he was taking teachers' training at the University of British Columbia. The dog had been left at the S.P.C.A. by a family who loved him, but felt he was not happy in the city, with the stipulation that he was to go to a farm. When Brian described the ranch to the man in charge, the dog was given to him and he had become an integral part of Windsong. There was a path worn through the grass around the house that he circled regularly on patrol, when he wasn't down in the meadow barking at gophers or chasing coyotes.

"Hi Silver!" Christopher sounded excited as he put down his lunch kit and threw his arms around the dog's neck. The dog

17

responded by licking the boy's face. Chris laughed in delight while rollicking with the dog around the yard. "Can Silver come with us tomorrow?"

"If we go, you mean."

"If we go, can Silver come, do you think? I'd like it if he did."

"Probably, we'll see."

"Oh good. You want to come, don't you Silver?" The dog took Christopher's hand in his mouth playfully as if in response to the question.

"He wants to come, Dad, look." Brian laughed as he walked towards the house and Chris followed.

2 Windsong

Brian never came home to Windsong without thinking of his grandfather Logan and the many hours they had spent there together. From his childhood came the recollection of his grandfather's voice telling him stories in such a vivid way that Brian felt that he had been there. He had listened to tales of the building of the railroad through the Kicking Horse Pass, his grandfather's part in the construction of the Spiral Tunnels, the ups and downs of the lumbering industry, and the mining in the area.

The roof of the house was made of thick, heavy shakes to hold the winter's snow. The log cabin with a stone fireplace was at one end of the house. When Brian built the new wing giving the house an L shape, he retained the original log dwelling for sentimental reasons towards his grandfather, more than for practical ones, and turned it into a family room off the kitchen which he modernized. He left the old structure just as it was. In the new wing, he put in three bedrooms, a living room, two sets of plumbing and added a basement. He covered the new section with siding that matched the old weathered logs. He installed sliding glass doors to a patio off the dining area between the family room and living room, allowing the occupants all the conveniences of a city dwelling with the beauty of the surrounding area as a bonus. The house was warm in winter and cool in summer as he had doubled the insulation.

The back of the house faced east where the glacial winds swept down from the Rockies over the long harsh winter. Therefore, the only windows were the ones needed for light. Christopher's bedroom window was on that side. A small bathroom window and the one above the kitchen sink had a view of the yard with the corral and barns. It was through this window that Sam observed the family within.

From the windows on the west was a spectacular view of the Columbia Valley where that majestic river flows and the Selkirk Mountains with their ever-changing hues, filled the beholders' eyes with the magnificence of this wilderness.

Chris and Brian entered the mud (or outer) room, where they removed their riding boots and jackets, and hung them in the closet. They put on slippers left there when they went out in the morning and went through the door into the large kitchen, brilliantly lit by the rays of the sun slowly abdicating reign to the shadows of the coming night.

The walls of the adjoining family room were covered with nine-and-a-half-inch wide knotted cedar that had been ordered by Cyrus and brought in by special order from Vancouver. The wood was arranged vertically and extended from the floor to the vaulted ceiling which allowed the family an exceptionally large tree at Christmas. The floor-to-ceiling, stone fireplace covered one end of the room, and stripped fir posts separated this room from the kitchen. Little wicker baskets hung on the posts from which ivy grew in profusion.

Chris walked over to the refrigerator and opened the door. "Oh boy, she left us hamburgers." He took out an apple and took a big bite. "Can we eat early, Dad?"

"Sure, if you want to, but right now you better change your clothes and start getting your things ready to go tomorrow, in case we decide to go."

"Do you think he's really gone?"

"He might be. He's been acting like he did other years just before he left, eating twice as much of my hay like he is storing up for a while."

"You should charge him rent, Dad," Chris said, laughing. "Wouldn't that be something if you could charge Sam rent? Oh boy, I sure hope we can go." He was getting a little excited from laughing and the thought of leaving in the morning, so he blurted unintentionally, "I already told Kevin that's what we are going to do this weekend, track Sam."

"So that's why you told Kevin about Sam. Had to go bragging, did you?"

"Well, Kevin talks about their camper and going fishing all the time, like he is the only one who can go away for the weekend. So I said we're going to track Sam this weekend to see where he goes, cause I thought it didn't matter. Sam was here this morning when we left for school and I didn't think he would go for sure."

"The only problem with that is, you know we can't have a bunch of people driving up here to see Sam and take pictures of him and all that. Besides, what if it got into the newspapers? I can see all the acclaim the papers would give it, and then all the nature lovers would be swarming up here with their cameras, city people getting stuck on the road, and maybe some jerk with a gun would spoil everyone's fun in hunting season. Sam is a wild sheep, and they can be hunted and shot in hunting season every fall, you know."

Chris was upset by what he had done but still tried to defend himself.

"But you told the game warden."

"I did it so he would help us protect Sam. I thought he should know he was here."

"I'm sorry, Dad."

"Okay, maybe no harm will come of it. Now go get changed and get some things ready to take tomorrow in case we go."

"What do I need do you think?"

"Some good warm things as it could get pretty cold up there at night, and something light for during the day if this weather holds."

"Okay." Chris went out into the hall and along to his room. He took a knapsack out of his closet and put it on his bed. Then he got jeans, socks, and a heavy sweater and put them by the knapsack. Christopher's thoughts distracted him from what he was doing so he wandered over to the window to look out where he could see the corral and the horses, but the ram, who was usually there where he could watch him, was missing. He rested his elbows against the window sill and put his face in his hands.

Chris had been thinking about his mother often of late, and as he rested his chin on his hands, the memory of her came into his mind and a look of longing to his eyes. He could see her face radiant and smiling as they stood together by the corral while a sheep with big horns looked at them. He could hear her soft voice saying, "He's your ram, darling. He came the day you were born. What do you want to call him?" And Chris answered, "Sam, I want to call him Sam the ram." They had laughed together, and his mother took him in her arms and kissed him, and he had seen her love shining in her eyes. A little sob escaped his lips, and the voice of his father calling from the kitchen broke the spell.

"What do you want on your hamburger?"

"Ketchup and cheese," Chris called as he scrambled to change his clothes, then dashed to the bathroom to wash his hands and on into the kitchen and straight to the fridge. Reaching for the handle to the freezing compartment, he turned to Brian.

"Can we have fries too?"

"Okay, get them and I'll put them in the oven, but you'll have to get the table ready.

"I will." Chris took a package of frozen fries from the freezer and poured some into a pan which he took to Brian who put it in the oven, before grabbing again for the metal spatula to rescue the searing patties as the grease from the over-heated pan splattered out onto the stove. Brian's lips formed words but no sound came, as for a fleeting moment he longed for the return of Hazel, the nanny, who cared for Chris and cooked their meals before he and Jennifer were married. Chris busied himself with setting the table with ketchup and mustard, and relish, all the things that he liked before taking the plates to Brian at the stove.

"When is Jennifer coming home?"

"She had to work late tonight." Brian frowned and looked at Chris as if to say something further, but he burned his hand on the frying pan just then, so he swore a bit under his breath before he asked, "Why are you calling her Jennifer again?" He looked at Chris who didn't answer. "Chris, why are you calling her Jennifer?"

"Because that's what I want to call her."

"But you were calling her 'Mom' before." Brian's voice was edged with concern.

"You said I could call her Jennifer if I want to."

"Hamburgers are ready." Brian sighed in resignation as he took the fries out of the oven and carried them to the table. The two sat down and started to devour the over-cooked food in silence, each lost in his own thoughts, until Chris, who had stopped eating to lick the ketchup off his fingers, asked, "If we go, are we taking the camera? I bet we could get some good pictures."

"If we go, we'll take the camera all right. It could be a chance for some good shots of the fall colors." He paused, looking at his son for a few minutes wondering if there was something seriously wrong with his relationship with Jennifer or just a childish notion that was best ignored. "How was school today?"

Chris finished chewing the mouthful of food he had just taken before answering. "It was all right. We live in the Rocky Mountains, don't we?"

"At the foot of the Rocky Mountains."

"The mountains touch heaven, don't they?"

"People say they do."

They continued their meal in silence. Brian became lost in his own thoughts, but Chris continued to watch him intently. Then he said, "I'll bet that is why Sam goes up into the mountains; he wants to see heaven." Brian was so deeply engrossed in his own thoughts that he failed to hear what Christopher had said. So the child, not having received any comment from his father, recalled to mind his father saying, "Mommy has gone to heaven."

After they had finished eating, Chris asked for a popsicle,

and Brian said, "Yes, if you take your dishes to the sink first." Which he did and then he went to the family room off the kitchen and turned on the television. Brian finished cleaning the table, then went over to a chair near Chris, sat down and picked up the book *Mountain Sheep and Man in the Northern Wilds*. He had just found his page and started to read when Chris wanted to have the fireplace on. Brian lowered his book long enough to see that Chris opened the draft before he put a match to the ready fire, and closed the screen as it burst into flame and the sparks flew as it crackled. He was getting nicely into reading where he left off when Chris drew his attention.

"Dad."

"Hmm."

"Do you think Jennifer would stay home if we asked her to?"

"She wants to come; why should she stay home?"

"Cause I want just you and me to go."

Brian studied his son's unrevealing face with a puzzled look on his own before he asked, "What's come over you, Chris? Don't you like Jennifer anymore?"

"I like her all right."

"Then what is it?" When Chris didn't answer he continued, "You wanted us to get married, everything was all right then." There was still no answer from the boy. "Has something happened between you two?" There was just that inscrutable look on his son's face, and his chin was pointing out further than normal, which Brian knew from past experience meant the end of the conversation, but he tried once more in a softer tone. "What is it, Chris?"

"I just don't want her to come with us to track Sam." Brian felt the muscles tighten in his stomach, which had been happening a lot lately in conversations with his child, so he said in annoyance, "Well, she's coming and that is final."

Brian had been reading about the "bachelor's club" of the bighorn rams. How they stuck together in groups of all males, and how they challenged each other by tilting their head to the side to show the size of their horns, a sign of distinction. No ram would challenge a ram with a set of horns larger than his own. Therefore, the ones with the smaller horns became subordinates.

He had been quite amused by this, but as he sat trying to concentrate on his reading, he found his thoughts and his eyes straying to his son who had lost interest in the program on television and was staring into the fire with a far away look of longing on his face. Brian had tried before to get Chris to say what was on his mind when he had seen this look on his face, but had got nowhere. He had gone through feelings of anger and despair as he tried to find out what went on in his child's mind. The story of the rams was lost to him as he sat staring into the fire reflecting on the past.

He wondered, as he had many times lately, if he had married again too soon, and felt the familiar feeling of guilt arise. He thought he was doing it for Chris at the time. Chris had been after him constantly to get him a new mother, and seeing his loneliness and not being able to bear his own, he complied with the boy's wishes, and now he wondered if it had been the right thing to do. After Joanne died, it was difficult for him in Golden, a teacher in a small town where the Logan family was highly respected. He was watched and talked about constantly. There wasn't anyone for him there, so when he went to Vancouver for the summer to finish his courses at UBC, and met Jennifer, it was like an answer to a prayer. He loved her on sight. Her soft way of speaking and gentle manner were a solace to his unhappiness. But a thought entered Brian's mind that he instantly wished had never come, that Jennifer did not love his son as if he were hers, or knew his every need. He remembered the first time he had heard her voice raised at Chris in anger. It was like a knife turning in his heart, creating a conflict within himself which divided his loyalty between his first and second wife, confusing him, resulting in loss of confidence in himself, and his newly created family. It was after they had come together that he trusted Jennifer to help him raise his son. He was surprised to find her needs as acute as his own. The realm of love spread in front of them. They approached it hand in hand, bashful and shy, approaching and withdrawing, approaching and falling, feasting and eddying and feasting again, then laying expounded, eyes staring, brown into blue, smiling, hearts pounding, breathless, communication so profound they had no need for words. And now the seeds of doubt were entering Brian's mind.

The electronic sound of the newscast jarred Brian back into reality, and the lateness of the hour. Chris should have been in bed long ago.

"Time for bed, Chris."

"Aw heck."

"Come on now, we have to get up early."

"Are we really going?" Chris moved reluctantly across the room to the door.

"We just might. That's if Sam doesn't come back tonight, but I think he has gone, because according to this book it will soon be the mating season. So you better get a good sleep." Brian was more determined than ever to take his son to follow the ram in hope of finding out what was at the bottom of his conflict with Jennifer, if that was the case, and the cold hand of fear touched his heart at the thought that after she had come to Windsong to live, Chris did not like her, after all.

"Goodnight, Dad. I sure hope we go."

"Goodnight."

After Christopher left the room, Brian tried to listen to the news, but the fact that Jennifer was not home was distracting him. The store where she worked was closed, so he couldn't think what could be keeping her. He knew she drove well enough in the city, but was not sure how well she handled the hill on the Trans Canada with the number of big trucks that rolled at night. He got up and paced around through the kitchen, watching for the car lights coming through the trees. Then, realizing what he was doing and the futility of it, he went back and sat in his chair and tried to concentrate on his book.

After Chris said goodnight to his father, he stopped in the bathroom long enough to tend to basic needs. No use brushing his teeth or washing when Dad was alone with him; he would forget to check, especially tonight; it seemed like Dad had a lot on his mind. When Chris reached his room he put on his pyjamas and climbed into bed and turned out his light. But he got up again and went to the window to check the sky to see if there were any clouds gathering to mar their trip. A harvest moon shone from a cloudless sky illuminating the yard as if it were daylight. He looked toward the corral and saw that Sam had not returned, and remembered the antics he had witnessed the night before. Sam was putting his head on one side and gesturing toward his Dad's horse, Glory, in a way Chris had not seen before, so he had stayed at the window to watch instead of just saying goodnight to Sam like he usually did. Looking at Sam helped him remember things about his mother, and he could fall asleep seeing her smiling face when she kissed him goodnight. He could even recall the sound of her voice when reading him bedtime stories like she often did. Jennifer didn't have much time for stories; she worked at the supermarket most nights and came home after he had gone to sleep. He saw the reflection of headlights coming through the bush and got quickly back into bed.

3   Life in the Country

Jennifer Logan got out of the car, picked up her bag of groceries, and hurried into the house. She was of medium height, somewhat on the plump side, as she enjoyed a variety of food and had little time for exercise. Her hair was long and shone bright red in the sun. And her large brown eyes, which radiated warmth, were the most attractive feature of her pretty face. Her skin was smooth and white except for a spattering of freckles across her nose that she was self-conscious about and went to great lengths to disguise. Her clothes had the distinction of the smart ladies' apparel shops in Vancouver that suited the pert way she held her head, and the polite little smile she gave to strangers. She walked with the quick gait of a person familiar with city crowds.

As she entered the kitchen, she saw Brian in his chair by the fire so she put the groceries on the counter and went to him and bent to kiss him.

"Hi honey."

"Hi." He lowered the book to receive her kiss. "How was your day?" Not waiting for her answer he continued, "It's late, I was getting worried about you."

"It was so busy I had to pick up my own things after they closed the store. Everybody in the country came in tonight. When it's a long weekend, people buy like there's no tomorrow. I brought home what I think we will need for the trip, so I had better get it put away." She went to the bags on the counter and started unpacking and putting things in the cupboard, asking as she worked, "Did Chris get to bed early?"

"Quite." Brian put the book down and stared into the fire with a pondering look on his face.

Jennifer watched him for a few minutes, apprehension growing, then she asked, "Is something wrong, Brian?"

"No, I guess not."

She watched him for a few minutes more, then said, "I think there is. What is it?"

"I can't figure out why Chris doesn't want you to come on the trip."

"He has been cool to me lately. I can't understand it either. He seems to have changed since he started school for some reason, and since he started pushing you to take him to see where Sam goes. It's almost as if he resents me being here. I hope I haven't done anything to hurt him."

"I don't see how you could have, you've been good to him. He wanted us to get married and it looked like he was starting to turn to you, and now this. I just don't understand it. Children are so complicated sometimes."

"This one is, it seems. He is so strong-willed and he keeps everything locked inside. He's hard to reach."

"I know. I'm not very good with him, I guess. I try, but when he gets that stubborn look on his face, and that pointed chin sticks out, I just give up."

Brian seemed to slump in his chair and Jennifer wanted to go to him, but she felt like she was the one who was being held responsible for his unhappiness, so in an uneasy voice she said, "I know what you mean." After contemplating for a few minutes, she remarked, "But you're not like that."

"No." Brian sighed as he continued, "His mother was; she was very determined." He paused for a minute remembering. "She fought hard against her illness, but it was no use. It was sad. I think she gave up towards the end because she thought it was affecting Chris."

Brian sat looking into the fire, lost in thought. Jennifer went back to the kitchen to unpack the groceries, and felt left out. She knew he was remembering Joanne, and wished he would tell her about the sorrow he kept locked inside. She hadn't known until after they were married that he hadn't got over her death. It had wedged a breach between them that she hoped could be overcome in time, but since the problem with Chris arose, the breach seemed to have widened, and her resentment toward Chris festered there. Hoping to distract him from his train of thought, she said from the kitchen, "It looks like we are going to have nice weather. The sky is all clear and the moon is shining. Sam was here when I left for work at noon, but I didn't see him when I came in. Would we be able to pick up his trail if he doesn't come back tonight?"

"I think we could pick up his trail easy enough. He's probably gone. He usually goes about this time of year, and he has been acting kinda excited like I've seen him do other years before he leaves, plus stuffing himself with hay. I hope he has gone; it would be a good time for us to go with the weather like it is and the long weekend. Better than if he left during the week and we couldn't get away to follow him. Chris would get pretty upset if that happened. He has been talking about this for weeks, and I pretty well committed myself to take him. If Sam hasn't returned by morning and the weather looks good, I think we should definitely go."

"What have you learned from the book?" Jennifer folded up the bags and put them under the sink before walking over to sit on the hearth facing Brian. She looked at his rugged face and thought, he's not stubborn, but he's strong. Every line of his face, from his receding brown hair with its bit of remaining curl, to the line of his jaw and the way he holds his head high above his broad shoulders showed strength. My rock of ages, she thought. She was about to go and lay her head on his lap and tell him about her visit to the doctor and the wonderful news she had received. She wondered if he would change his mind about making the trip. Fearing he may think it best for her to stay at home, she said nothing. Then she heard him saying, "It should be getting close to the rutting season, like I thought, and I do think that's where he goes. He probably had a fight

30

with another ram and lost, that's why he came here in the first place, but he came in the spring. Maybe he was chased by coyotes or something. It doesn't say anything here about them fighting other than rutting season. I don't know. I had quit wondering why he came and just accepted him being here till Chris got this idea of following him."

Jennifer didn't understand the deep feeling Brian and Chris, especially Chris, had for the sheep. She thought it had something to do with their roots. They were both raised close to nature while she grew up in the city, and had very little appreciation of wild and natural things. She hoped to learn, as she wanted to enjoy nature, like Brian and Chris did. But at present she hated the ram as she held him responsible for her exclusion from the deep bond between the father and son.

She saw the worried look coming back on Brian's face so she said, "We better start getting our gear together. Will you go downstairs and get the sleeping bags?" Brian got up and started for the hall.

"Where do you want them?" he asked.

"In the mud room at the top of the stairs, so it will be easier in the morning."

Brian came up from the basement with his arms loaded with camping equipment and deposited it by the door. He went down for a second load and put it on the floor by the first, then knelt and sorted it: sleeping bags, riding boots, saddle bags, flashlights, and a little tent. He took a list he made out earlier from his pocket and crossed off the items. He was being meticulous he knew, but he didn't want to forget anything, not this time, not with Chris and Jennifer along. Chris was pretty good in the wilds; they had been out before, but Jennifer hadn't and he wanted to make sure he had what they needed in case of a crisis; you never know in the mountains, anything could happen. He came to the bottom of the list and saw where he had written "gun," so he got up and went into the family room and took the rifle off the rack on the wall by the fireplace. He opened the little drawer under the gun rack, took out a kit and sat down to clean the gun.

Jennifer was assembling things in the kitchen like mugs, a

31

thermos, and unbreakable plates. She started when she saw Brian take the gun down. She hated guns, never having had them around in her life before, and tried not to look at Brian's gun rack on the wall. She had almost forgotten it was there until he took his rifle down. She said, "You're not taking that, are you?"

"Yes." Then seeing her reluctance he said, "This is wild country we are going into, Jennifer. You never know what we might run into. We may need it for protection." He saw the look of fear come into her eyes and almost said, "Are you sure you want to come?" but didn't. Instead he said, "You have got to understand that guns are a part of the way of life in this country. They are used more for protection than for destruction." He was trying not to show his annoyance at her, as this was not the first time her dislike of guns had come up.

"Maybe you think it's necessary to destroy animals for protection, but that's not always so. You use your gun because you have it, when there is no real danger anyway."

"That's not true," Brian answered defensively. "I used my gun to save the colt and Silver's life one night. I heard a terrible commotion down in the meadow and ran down there, straight over the bank from the house. I didn't have time to go by the road. Five coyotes had Silver and the colt backed against the cliff. Silver was protecting the colt, up in the corner of the pasture against the cliff. I got there just in time. The coyotes were ready to move in for the kill, as both Silver and the colt were exhausted. I fired my gun in the air, and the coyotes ran off. The colt was covered in sweat and its heart was pounding so hard I could see it in the moonlight. I brought Silver up to the house after I put the colt in the barn. His collar was nearly bitten through. It was covered with teeth marks, and his heavy licence tag was chewed up but that's probably what saved him, that and his heavy collie coat." What he didn't tell her was that he had run down there in the middle of a cold February night in his boots and undershorts, through four feet of snow.

He paused for a few minutes, remembering. He knew by the look on her face that she hadn't understood any of what he had said, and wondered what he had expected from a girl whose only experience with wild animals had been in Vancouver at Stanley Park. So he gave up in exasperation and said, "I've done about all I can for tonight; I think I'll hit the sack," and started for the door.

"Okay, I won't be long," she said, the disappointment that he was going to bed and leaving her sounding in her voice. Jennifer went back to getting things ready in the kitchen and Brian went down the hall to their room. She was feeling disappointed in the way the evening had gone. She had been so happy all day, and when she came home she had wanted to tell Brian about it, but he had been so concerned with Chris and the trip that she hadn't been able to talk to him at all about the things she wanted to; so she hurried in the kitchen hoping his mood would change and they could have a few tender moments in bed together before they went to sleep. But when she entered their room later, she knew he was already sound asleep, so she got into bed and turned out the light and snuggled as close to him as she could.

She had been happily anticipating going home at the end of her shift, as well as the prospect of the trip into the mountains for the weekend. It wasn't exactly what she would have chosen to do if she had been asked, but seeing as Brian did what Chris wanted she had to either go along or stay home by herself. Jennifer lay awake thinking of her day.

It was busy in the store and she was making change for the customer she was serving whom she didn't recall ever having seen before when he spoke.

"I'm Greg Logan, Brian's cousin." At first she was upset at not remembering him, thinking they had met at the reception that Brian's mother and father had for them when they were first married, but the man spoke again before she apologized for not recognizing him. "Don't worry, we haven't met." She was relieved and then resentful, for he was giving her the same look of comparison they all did at first. His scrutiny was so keen she was becoming very annoyed and was on the point of asking him how she compared to Brian's first wife, when he went on. "I was out of town when uncle had the reception for you and Brian. We live up in Spillimacheen. We're on our way to Calgary for the weekend, so we thought we'd stop here for supplies for the camper. How do you like living at Windsong?" he asked, noticing her sleek city appearance.

"I love it," she lied.

Jennifer was glad she had learned a few things since coming to Golden, like Spillimacheen was an Indian word for "swift running water."

"We are planning on going heli-skiing in the Bugaboos this winter and Brian says we may fly up from Spillimacheen."

"Well, say hello to Brian for me and stop in and see us if you're up our way."

This encounter made Jennifer feel even more out of her element, so totally out of step with the one she had been used to. She remembered that after Brian asked her to marry him he told her about his family background, about his grandfather Logan and the tales he had spun. She found them fascinating at the time, but that was in the comfort of familiar surroundings. And she wondered now if Brian was trying to prepare her for the life she was going to be a part of.

Most of the stories were of how they had suffered the hardships that befell all the early settlers of the Kootenays in Eastern British Columbia. Long hard winters when the temperature dropped below zero, and the snow fell and drifted over the roads and fences where it remained until April or May. Late springs, when rivers and creeks overflowed their banks and covered the land, leaving a short season for growing. Hot dry summers, thick with mosquitoes, and forest fires that threatened not only their homes but their livelihood as well. And the ever-present threat of accident or illness with the closest doctor a day away by horse back. It took a hardy stock to survive.

The Logans were still a "rough and ready" pioneer people who loved their ranches, horses, and their children with equal depth. While Jennifer's life in the city had been centered around the pursuit of a career in music. Her father was an accountant for a large firm in Vancouver, and her mother filled her days with the business of the Opera Society and Kerrisdale luncheons.

34

She was an only child of middle-aged parents, and learned early that in exchange for doing well at her singing and piano lessons, her parents succumbed to her every whim.

Jennifer had wanted for nothing. Her parents made sacrifices in order to give their child the opportunity to have a career in music. Her mother, who sang equally well, had been denied the privilege. Therefore, Jennifer had all the comforts of a young lady well brought up in the heart of one of Vancouver's most affluent neighborhoods. It left her ill-prepared for the life on a ranch in B.C.'s rugged Columbia Valley.

Since coming to Golden to live and hearing of the severity of some of their winters from the people she met in the store, she wondered how she would survive, and had clung to the hope that it was still several months away. But now this trip into the mountains loomed and she had a foreboding that the hardships they would encounter, which were foreign to her, would alienate her further from Brian and Chris, and would show her as an intruder in their midst. She grew more hateful of the ram and the ranch, and her own lack of experience.

Thinking of Brian's relatives started her on a chain of resentments, and on top of the list was her growing jealousy of Chris, and the way he came first with Brian instead of her as she expected. In some of her most dire moods and only in her innermost thoughts, she had started thinking he was a spoiled, selfish brat. She had, at times, wondered how long she could stand it. Things had to change. She wished with all her heart that the trip to see where Sam goes would never take place. She knew she needed sleep for they were planning on rising early to decide if they would make the trip, so she moved away from Brian and turned her back to him. Her last wish was to awaken to pouring rain and then remembered she was in Golden, not Vancouver, and fell into a heavy sleep.

No city noises were heard here, only a lonely coyote howling off in the woods somewhere broke the stillness of the night. The temperature dropped to near freezing and a gentle breeze rose to whisper in the trees and send the dying leaves fluttering to the ground.

4   The Journey Begins

A faint light appeared above the mountain tops announcing the coming of dawn to the valley. The horses roused themselves from the ground where they had been lying, and the dog wandered out from his house under a pine, yawned and stretched, then strolled over to the house and sat on the step to greet the first person venturing into the frosty dawn.

The lights came on in the house, and Jennifer was in the kitchen making coffee when Chris wandered in wearing his pyjamas. "What's for breakfast?" he asked, while rubbing sleep from his eyes.

"Oh, I think we are going to have a big breakfast this morning. How would you like ham and eggs and hashbrowns?" she told him, feigning cheerfulness.

Before Chris could answer, Brian came in from outside, all smiles, and announced, "Sam has gone. He didn't come back during the night."

"Are you sure, Dad?" Chris asked with excitement in his voice, "Are you sure he's gone?"

"Seems to be; he's not in the corral with the horses, or down in the meadow by the pond, I checked, or anywhere else around the ranch, so I guess he's gone all right."

"Can we go, Dad? Can we go after him?" Chris was beside himself with excitement.

Brian looked at Jennifer, and said, "Well, what do you think?"

"It looks like it's going to be another beautiful day, so why not."

"Boy, oh boy, we're going, we're really going to track Sam!" Chris was hopping around the room in his excitement. His hopes and dreams were going to come true at last, and he was beside himself with joy.

"Hey, calm down. You better go and get dressed. We should get started right after breakfast." Brian went over to Jennifer and gave her a kiss. "I'll get the packs ready, so give me a call when breakfast is ready, will you?"

Jennifer said she would, but it would be a while as she wanted to fill the thermos with coffee and make sandwiches for lunch first. When Chris offered to help, she told him to scoot along to his room and get dressed, and then he could give her a hand if she needed it.

When Chris and Jennifer came out of the house after breakfast all dressed in their riding clothes, Brian had the three horses saddled and ready to go and the pack horse loaded. Glory, a high-spirited Arabian bay with a white star on her forehead, was prancing around, impatient to be off on the journey for which she was saddled. Jingle, Christopher's pony, a palomino, like his mother who stood with her head over the fence watching, was tossing his white mane and tail waiting for his rider to appear. Bess, a gentle sorrel, stood quietly undisturbed by the goings on around her.

Brian was amused at the way Silver had been wandering around the corral watching every move while he was getting the horses saddled and Nelliebell, the pack horse, loaded. He saw him run to meet Chris and Jennifer when they came out of the house, with his tail wagging in anticipation, but they were in a hurry and other than a quick "hi" didn't pay any attention to him. Brian knew he must have sensed that they were all going somewhere, for the preparations were more elaborate than any there had been at Windsong for a long time. The extensive packing along with the missing ram was bound to have the dog excited. Brian had patted the dog's head when he first came out of the house at the crack of dawn, but no one had said anything to Silver about going along and it was obvious that he was getting a little uneasy about it. He decided a little coaxing was in order and started a little game of tag with Chris, by circling around him. When that didn't work he brushed up against him and ran in front of him a bit, but nothing seemed to deter the boy from his headlong march towards his horse, whose neck he patted before climbing on. Brian saw the dog's head droop a bit in disappointment when Chris got on his horse without noticing his antics and knew just how he was feeling.

There wasn't anything Silver disliked more than being left behind when his family went somewhere. He even tolerated the car which he obviously hated, just to go along. The truck was a little better for him as he could ride in the back and let the wind blow in his face. But when they went out with the horses and Brian had to tell him he couldn't go, he got a heart-broken look in his eyes and slinked off to the house with his tail between his legs and his head sunk to his chest. Christopher's horse stepped around a bit as soon as he was firmly in the saddle and Brian saw Silver's head droop even lower, but his ears perked up when he heard Chris speak.

"Is Silver coming?" Brian looked at Silver and saw his heart in his eyes, and then at Jennifer who said, "I thought he might be coming so I stuck in a few cans of dog food just in case."

"Okay," Brian said.

"Come on Silver, you're coming too." Chris started riding his horse around the yard while Silver followed with his head high and his tail going from side to side.

There was an eerie light in the cold air of early dawn when the three of them mounted up and rode off toward the same stand of trees where the ram had gone the day before.

As they rode away from Windsong, it was evident that Jennifer was an inexperienced rider by the way she sat on her horse, and it remained to be seen if it was courage or lack of knowledge that prompted her to venture forth on a horse for a day's ride. It was obvious that the horse knew that she was nervous for it showed signs of doing as it pleased and therefore lingered behind. Brian and Chris, on the other hand, rode with the confidence that comes from many hours spent in the saddle. They moved with the animals as if they were one. The horses in turn knew their masters and leaned to their wishes. It was as if no visible handling was taking place between horse and rider, an unseen communication was going on. Silver stayed close to Christopher's horse.

When they reached the edge of the clearing above Windsong, Brian turned in his saddle and looked at the ranch spread below. He recalled a glorious summer day when he was a boy and was off for a day's ride in the mountains with his Grandfather Cyrus. They had stopped at this same spot to admire the view of the ranch as they always did before entering the bush and leaving the spectacular sight behind. Cyrus had been telling Brian about an unusual engineering experience he had in some far away place when Brian asked, "When I get to be an engineer like you Grandpa, will I have to go away from Windsong too?"

"Yes, you will have to travel to where the work is, traveling is very interesting and you can come home in between jobs." Cyrus said, amused.

"Then I'm not going to be an engineer. I don't want to leave here and travel. I'm not going to be a lawyer like Daddy either because they never have time to do things with their kids. I'm going to be a teacher like Mr. Elliot so I can stay here and do things."

Cyrus had laughed, but all the persuading he had done over the years had never changed Brian's mind. And when Brian was attending university in Vancouver he couldn't wait to finish, so he could return to Golden. He loved the mountains; he felt that there was something about their majesty that sanctioned life, and when he told this to his grandfather he had agreed with him.

When Cyrus had died, Brian missed him sorely. He realized that his father was like a stranger to him, and he became determined not to let it be that way between himself and Christopher.

When they came to the creek, they startled a deer who was drinking, and it bounded off into the bush. Jennifer almost fell from her horse in fright at her first sight of this beautiful wild animal in its natural habitat. "I'm going to love this," she lamented. Both males looked at her without comment, sights like this being nothing unusual to them.

Brian dismounted and looked along the soft bank of the creek until he saw the tracks the ram had made when he went that way after being rejected by the horses. "It looks like Sam followed the creek all right, so that's what we're going to have to do too," he told them as he got back on Glory.

As they rode on in the early morning chill, Brian was in the lead with the pack horse, Chris rode in the middle and Jennifer behind Chris. They were silent for a time, each watching his or her horse step carefully over logs and rocks on the rough terrain. When they came out of the bush, the sun was starting to peep over the mountains and cast its rays over the valley below, but they were still in shadow. No sun was touching the west slope of the mountains or shining on the bushes dressed in their autumn leaves, but Jennifer recognized the area as the one where they had hiked to last summer, which seemed like a long way from home at the time, to pick huckleberries for her to make jam; now she was surprised how close it was to the ranch. All that remained on the bushes were some crimson leaves and they too would soon be gone.

The memory of that happy day when she was still somewhat of a bride was a treasured one with Jennifer, and she reflected on it now. How happy she had been, how much fun they all had, the laughter they shared, and the contest to see who could pick the most berries before they ate their fill, and sat in the shade eating sandwiches and dousing their parched throats with cold beer. Her life had seemed so full then. They were becoming the family she wanted them to be.

Her anxiety over marrying a man who already had a son was abating, and her desire to comfort them with her love as wife and mother was filling her being.

Their loneliness when she first met them had been heart-rending. She looked at them riding ahead of her. Brian, with his broad straight back, his ease in the saddle, moving like he and the horse were one, and Chris behind was a carbon copy of his father, with that same proud Logan carriage. She had seen it in

Brian's stately father and his uncles when they came from Alberta for a visit. She wanted to belong and be one of them. She was sure this was why she had not married sooner. This was what she had been waiting for, waiting until she was thirty years old to marry for the first time, when there had been many opportunities, saying it was that one early disappointing affair that had hurt her when it had only taught her that there were better things. When she met Brian, she knew that this was what she had been waiting for.

The riding became easier for Jennifer as they crossed a slope covered with low-lying shrubs and old stumps where a fire once burned, as there were no branches to scratch her face and snag her long hair. Chris kept glancing back at her now and then, and she wondered if it was to see if she was all right or hoping that she were lost. She wondered about this child she had promised to help raise. He seemed eager for them to get married, and asked if he could call her Mom before the wedding day was set. She had been thrilled at the time, but now she wondered what he had expected of her. Not to walk in his mother's footsteps she hoped, as she was determined not to walk in a shadow. She wanted to make a place here of her own, one that included Brian and Chris and a child between her husband and herself. A little girl, perhaps, that would bring them all closer together, and make them a stronger family unit like the Logans, whom she admired.

All seemed to be going well before Chris got this incessant idea that he and Brian should follow the ram to see where he went, and the puzzling part of not wanting her along. He must have elaborated on it last night to Brian, and Brian was worried about it when she came home. He didn't want to talk about it either and that made her feel left out. She wasn't going to have Brian and Chris doing everything together while she stayed home and did the cooking and laundry. More in anger than in knowledge she spurred the horse on; it suddenly paid heed and moved faster and Jennifer had to grab hold of the saddle horn to stay on.

They came to a place where the creek made a small canyon through the rocks, and the walls of the little canyon rose up on either side leaving no room for the riders. They had to leave the creek and skirt around the canyon over a rock slide, making it necessary for them to dismount and lead their horses across the treacherous rocks.

She was having difficulty with the rocks, not knowing which ones were stable or which ones would tip over with her weight. She had the added burden of watching that the horse made the correct choice as well. Several times she stepped on a loose rock and nearly fell, causing her ankles to twist painfully and the horse to stumble. Brian called to her to be more careful if she didn't want her horse to become lame and have to return home. At that point she was annoyed at her own incompetence and the obstacles ahead looked too much for her, so she asked, "Would it please you more if I returned home?" Without realizing that she had spoken in anger, Brian said nothing, but Chris suggested that it wasn't far if that was what she wanted, with a look of disgust on his face at her inadequacy. And she, remembering that was exactly what he wanted her to do, became determined to carry on. They reached the safety of the grassy slope beyond the rock slide and ascended a steep incline that brought them again in contact with the creek.

Brian reached the top of the bank first so he stopped and waited for the others to catch up. Then he said they should leave their horses there and follow him. They climbed over some large rocks that brought them out on to a ledge above the little canyon that the creek had made, and at this particular spot they could see all the way down to the valley below and the mountains on the other side, where the town of Golden nestled between the Rocky Mountains and Selkirk range.

Jennifer was surprised at how high they had climbed, but she was too angry over the rebuff she had received from Brian and Chris at the rock slide to appreciate the beauty of the valley spread in panoramic splendor. Brian started to whistle. It was shrill and seemed to bounce off the rocky bluffs ahead and echo all the way down to the valley below. "I want to do that too," Chris said.

So Brian showed him how to cup his hands together and make an opening between his thumbs, put his mouth on his thumbs, and blow, as he moved his outside hand back and forth to create that shrill vibrating sound that seemed to bounce and roll and echo forever. Chris was thrilled. Pleasure was registered all over his face.

"I'll bet you can't do that, Jennifer," he said with a grin, forgetting for the moment that he wanted her to stay home. "I don't think I'll even try."

"Oh come on it's not hard, try," Brian said teasingly. So she came up beside them and cupped her hands to her mouth and yelled in a sing-song voice, "You hoo." It rolled on down the valley and seemed to come back at them, you hoo. So she sang, "In the valley you hoo," then after the echo rolled away she sang, "there's an echo, you hoo, and it's saying I love you I do." They all laughed as the echo died away and Brian said, "That sounds like an oldie."

"A moldy oldie," giggled Chris.

"Oh, probably; I can't even remember where I heard it. One of my music courses, I guess."

Jennifer felt a bit better, some of the tension had gone, as they turned and climbed down the rocks to the waiting horses, after Brian had suggested that they had better be on their way and Chris said, "Yeah, we gotta catch up to Sam."

They mounted and rode on along the bluff, and entered deep bush beyond. It was still cool in the shade so she shivered, after being in the first welcome rays of the morning sun as it had burst upon them on the bluff before they entered the woods and the pungent odor of musty leaves reached their nostrils. The music from an old tune started going through her mind. The words followed, "Lonely woods with paths dim and silent, a haunt of peace for weary hearted, there's healing in your shade, and in your stillness balm." She couldn't understand how anyone could find solace in the damp gloom of anything like the forests of British Columbia; maybe they were different in Europe, where the music was probably composed.

It seemed to Jennifer that they had been riding through the woods for hours, and she couldn't picture where they were, not having seen a stand of timber such as the one they were in from the ranch. But then she didn't know east from west or north from south either. For the first time in her life she knew how it felt to be lost, and was glad that she was not alone. First they were riding up an incline and then they were riding down again. She wanted to stop and rest, but there was nowhere suitable. It was damp and cold among the trees and she longed for the sunshine again, when she noticed the trees were thinning out and it looked brighter ahead. When they finally emerged from the woods they were greeted by sunshine, which pleased her, and they were by the creek again, but it was larger and she was curious, so she asked, "How come the creek is so much bigger?"

"Because it's not the creek, it's the river and it looks like that's the way Sam is headed, which is good for us since the going will be easier," Brian explained.

They were on a grassy bank; the sun was shining and Jennifer wanted to rest. "Couldn't we stop here for a bit? I could use a rest and a cup of coffee."

"Sounds like a good idea to me." Brian swung his leg over and dismounted. But Chris didn't like the idea.

"No, I want to keep going. We haven't caught up to Sam yet."

"But, Chris, Jennifer needs to rest."

"I don't care, I want to catch up to Sam first." Chris nudged his horse to keep going, but Brian grabbed Jingle's bridle and made him stop.

"Now get off." When Chris reluctantly obeyed, Brian walked over to where Silver was sniffing in the soft earth at the side of the river, while Jennifer hurriedly got out mugs and thermos. "Look, Chris, these are Sam's footprints and they look fairly fresh, right." Chris nodded his head, so Brian continued, "That means he is not very far ahead, and I feel like a cup of coffee."

Jennifer was relieved to be out of the saddle, but Chris was still showing some reluctance which was annoying Brian, she could see; so she offered him a can of juice which he accepted, and then suggested that they sit on an old log and rest for just a few minutes so she could get her second wind. Chris found this amusing enough to almost smile.

While they sat in the warm sun on the bank of the river drinking the hot coffee, they started to relax. Brian told them this was the famous Kicking Horse River that played such a big part in the development of the railroad through the Kicking Horse Pass from Banff through the Rocky Mountains to Golden. Jennifer loved history almost as much as she loved listening to Brian talk, and Christopher loved a story, so they sat quietly while Brian related the history of the coming of the railroad to Vancouver with no interruptions from his audience, with the exception of Silver barking off in the woods after he treed a squirrel.

"When they first built the railroad there was a long climb up to the divide that was called the Big Hill. Sometimes it took four or five locomotives to pull the trains up, besides a lot of precautions which had to be taken to ensure the safety of the passengers and equipment. Just after the turn of the century the railroad was getting a lot of use, so they decided something had to be done to eliminate the Big Hill.

"They had to add several miles of track and build two more bridges across the Kicking Horse River, but they lowered the grade to about half, and also cut the number of required locomotives in half. Grandfather told me about it many times. I think it was the most rewarding feat of engineering he was ever engaged in. When I was a boy he used to tell me about it in such a way that I could understand. He wouldn't give up until I was thoroughly impressed and knowledgeable.

"They really eliminated a lot of the danger by building the tunnels. Before that they had more than one runaway train that resulted in tragedy. What happens with the tunnels is, coming from the east, the train enters the western Corkscrew tunnel under Cathedral Mountain. When it emerges from the tunnel twist, it runs back east across the Kicking Horse River and enters the eastern spiral tunnel under Mount Ogden. After an elliptical curve, it comes out and crosses the Kicking Horse again going westwards. Grandpa always described it as a perfect maze. The railroad doubles back upon itself twice, under the mountains, and crosses the river twice in order to cut down the grade.

"I remember Grandpa saying that they hired 1000 men and moved 650,000 cubic yards of rock to build two tunnels, one and a quarter miles long and seven miles of cutting outside. They increased the tracks by over four miles."

"Sounds absolutely fascinating." Jennifer had almost enjoyed it. It was relaxing sitting in the sun listening to Brian talk about his grandfather's great contribution to the building of the railroad. "You remember it well, the statistics, I mean."

"I heard it often enough. Grandpa was determined to make me into an engineer when none of his sons followed him. I broke his heart for a while when I went into teaching, and it bothered me a lot, but I think he forgave me some when Chris was born; he got his hopes up for an engineer in the family all over again. One more thing Grandpa always had to impress me with was that they used seventy-five carloads of dynamite while building the tunnels."

"I'm impressed, but I can't picture seventy-five carloads of dynamite." Jennifer could have sat there all day on the grassy bank by the river soaking up the sun. She had a good book that she was reading in her pack, but Chris had lost interest in the story Brian had told them long before it was finished, and was showing signs of impatience. She hated to leave, but said nothing.

When they got up to go and Jennifer started towards Bess, the horse turned and proceeded to go back down the trail the way they had come. Brian was beside her instantly, grabbing the reins and jerking them in anger, making Bess turn around in the direction they were going. "What's wrong with her?" Jennifer asked innocently.

"Oh, you are a such a pushover, she thinks she can go home. She will, too, and you will be walking," Brian said in anger and disgust.

"Well, how am I supposed to know how to handle a horse?" Jennifer asked peevishly.

"You can learn, can't you, for gosh sakes, or maybe you can't." He stomped off to mount Glory, and rode off leaving Jennifer to suffer Christopher's accusing looks, before he too turned and rode away. Jennifer managed to pull herself up into the saddle without any assistance from Brian for the first time. "I can learn if you'll just give me time," she said, but Brian and Christopher were already out of hearing range.

5   An Unexpected Lunch Guest

Christopher Logan handled a horse very well for a young boy and he loved to ride. Having inherited his great grandfather's spirit of adventure, it was his little pony who took him where he most wanted to go. He also loved his horse Jingle who had been given to him for Christmas and was the colt of his mother's mare. His father said he had picked the name himself after asking his mother what her horse's name was, and she had said "Bell," so when his father asked again what he wanted to name his horse he said, "Jingle, like Mommy's."

He had learned to sing "Jingle Bells" that year. He had also heard his Dad tell people who remarked how well he rode "that he had been practically born on a horse." And Chris thought that was because of the pictures he saw in the album at home of his mother, sitting on her horse holding a little baby in her arms, and his Dad said it was him. He also remembered seeing some movies of his Dad riding Glory around in the yard with him sitting in front holding on to the saddle horn. He looked pretty small then sitting on that big horse in front of Dad, but he could recognize his face.

He glanced back at Jennifer and saw that she was coming along slowly. He really wished she had stayed home. It was going to make it more difficult for him later on, having her along, and he didn't quite know what he was going to do about it. Then he thought maybe he would talk Dad into asking her to stay at the place where they spent the night to watch their food and stuff, while he and Dad went on ahead to follow Sam.

Chris had a bad feeling inside about Jennifer. She had been nice to him, and he thought about when they were having something to drink by the river and he was in a hurry to get going so they could catch up to Sam when the story his Dad was telling was getting too long. Dad was kind of angry with him when he said "Let's go, I want to get going," but Jennifer had jumped up and gathered the thermos and things and put them away in a hurry, and brought out some apples and said, "Here, let's eat these along the way; that will tie us over 'til lunch time."

As Jennifer handed Chris the apple he noticed her face was getting red, and there was a smudge of dirt on her cheek. She looked tired, and the day was not half over, so in a moment's sympathy and knowing she liked to sing, he asked, "Jennifer, will you sing us a song?"

Jennifer was a bit taken by surprise by Christopher's request, but the fact that he had shown an interest in her or had at least acknowledged that she was there pleased her, so she asked, "What would you like to hear?"

"Mm, how about Humpty Dumpty?" Chris asked in jest, while shaking his head from side to side.

"Don't be silly," Jennifer answered. "If you would really like to hear a song, then name one. Or, better yet, think of something we can all sing, and it will help to pass the time."

"Who needs to pass time?" Brian turned around and asked.

"Okay, big shot." Jennifer wrinkled up her nose at him but he was probably too far away to see, but she had the satisfaction of doing it anyway. She was pleased that they were civil to her again after how angry they had been when Bess started for home.

"First will you sing that scouts' song you learned when you were a little girl, about the beaver's home?" As Chris asked, he took a last big bite of his apple and dropped the core on the ground as they rode around a bend in the river. Unseen by the riders, a black bear ambled out of the bush and scooped up the apple core with a swoop of his huge paw, and put it in his mouth. He stood on his hind legs for a minute sniffing the air and then headed along the river behind the riders.

Jennifer was all set to burst into song with "Land of the silver birch, home of the beaver" but when she opened her mouth, no sound came. She was just too upset to sing. "My throat is too dry, Chris. I'll sing it later," and her anger at Brian for his impatience over her riding returned.

Brian had been looking forward to the trip all week as a release from the pressures of teaching, and he hoped to find a solution to the problem between Jennifer and Chris. He regretted his outburst at Chris for being impatient to get going, and his words with Jennifer when her horse started going home. He hated the feeling of uncertainty that had come over him lately. It made him irritable. Family conflicts upset him. They were almost nonexistent in his previous marriage.

Thinking Jennifer had an even temperament and would be easy to get along with, had been one of the things that had attracted him to her. But the anger that had shown in her voice when she spoke puzzled him, and he wondered how he had offended her so deeply.

Brian turned in his saddle and saw that she had pushed off her hat, and it was hanging on her back from the tie around her neck. A soft breeze was playing with her long brown hair, that looked bright red in the morning sun. He glimpsed the whiteness of her skin against her dark jacket from the distance between them, and knew that a warm light was shining in her deep brown eyes. Something inside him stirred and a strong desire to take her in his arms followed. But at that moment her horse stumbled over a piece of log, and instead of holding the rein firm and pulling the horse's head up, she let go and nearly fell off. Brian had been teaching her how to ride around the yard at the ranch and suspected that she did not take it seriously.

As she went from one blunder to another he felt it was lack of interest in the way of life he loved rather than inexperience with a horse. He spoke more sharply than he intended, "How many times do I have to tell you to hold the reins firm and keep the horse's head up?"

Jennifer, who had been very frightened by her near disaster, matched his tone with an equally blatent voice, "What do you expect of me, anyway? I wasn't born in this damn wild country like you were." Hearing that her voice ended on a tearful note, Brian swallowed the next harsh words that were ready on his lips, not wanting to make a scene in front of Chris. They rode for miles along the banks of the Kicking Horse River surrounded by the beauty that only an Indian summer day in the Canadian Rockies can display. The sun was high enough in the sky for its rays to warm the riders, and Jennifer was ready to stop for lunch and remove her jacket, but it looked to her like the two in front of her could ride on forever the way they were both just "rolling with the horse," as she had heard them say. They never seemed to tire. That's what it's like when you are born in the saddle, she thought, and wondered how long it took to reach that plateau as she was becoming a little sore where she sat.

She just couldn't seem to catch on to the knack of riding, as she was terrified of falling off. It was still a shock to her each time Brian boosted her up to the saddle to see how far it was to the ground, and she wanted to cling to the saddle horn to stay on. But seeing the look of annoyance on Brian's face when she did so after telling her she would never learn to ride that way, she refrained from doing it in his presence. She sat still and tense; therefore, she bounced up and down and was becoming both tired and saddle sore. Christopher's horse lifted its tail and relieved itself right in front of Jennifer, and it surprised her that horses could do this without warning or stopping. But the stench from the droppings was so offensive to her that she cringed in revulsion. And she wondered how long she could maintain the pretence of liking a way of life she found hideous.

They had been traveling for miles along the river, up what looked to her to be a valley. She took a deep breath of the pure fresh air with the scent of pine. It relieved her feeling of weariness, but her hunger pangs remained, so she called out to Brian and Chris who were a bit ahead of her, as her horse, having sensed her reluctant mood and the loosening of her hands on the rein, had lagged behind.

51

"Isn't anyone getting hungry?" she asked, not caring if they did get annoyed at her after Brian's last outburst.

Brian stopped his horse and looked at his watch. "I could use some lunch now that you mention it."

"We haven't caught up to Sam yet," Chris said petulantly, while keeping his horse moving.

"I'm sure he's just up ahead, Chris, and this is a good place to stop. The horses can graze on the grass and the river is shallow so they can drink. Besides, this is Jennifer's first big trip, and we don't want to wear her out the first day." He smiled at her as if he knew she was already getting saddle sore. Brian dismounted, blocking Christopher's way; so he had to stop and get off too. As he did, he gave Jennifer a look that made her think, "I'm back in his bad books again." So she hurriedly got the lunch out of her saddle bag as Brian took the reins of her horse, and led them to the river while Chris followed with Jingle. After the horses drank long and thirstily, they started nibbling on the grass by the river while Brian and Chris went and sat on the dry grass beside Jennifer to have their lunch. The males, who found they were hungry after all, ate hungrily from the mound of sandwiches spread before them.

When Jennifer poured herself a cup of coffee and then leaned over to pour what little remained in the thermos in Brian's cup, he remarked, "That's it for the coffee, I guess," making her annoyed at their constant demands upon her for their food. I'm turning into the Logan's version of "Meals on Wheels," rather "Meals on Horse," she thought.

"No, I have another thermos full; you know I can't get along without my coffee." They sat quietly sipping from the steaming mugs and soaking up the sun, and then Jennifer asked, "How far do you think we have come?"

"Well, let's see, I would say we have traveled about ten miles or sixteen kilometres, and as to how far from home we are as the crow flies, not very far."

At that point Chris couldn't help but suggest again, "You could go back easy if you want to, Jennifer." But they chose to ignore him.

"What were those cabins we passed this morning, just up

52

above Windsong a bit? I thought I caught a glimpse of one or two old cabins in the trees. Were they used by trappers or prospectors or something?"

"No." Brian sounded amused at her ignorance thinking trappers' cabins would be that low down on the mountain. "They were used by bootleggers during prohibition."

"Bootleggers!" Jennifer was surprised.

"Yes, as a matter of fact one of the Logans was involved." Knowing as she did that the Logans were a greatly respected pioneer family around Golden, hearing that one of them had been involved in bootlegging came to her as a bit of a shock which showed in her voice when she asked, "Who?" wondering if the offender was related to the Logan who had been in the store on Friday. Brian laughed and said, "It's a long story." Chris interrupted by asking, "When do you think we'll catch up to Sam?"

"Maybe this afternoon. And I had better leave the telling of the black sheep of the Logan family to another time. There is a wild sheep that this family is concerned about right now, and we should be on our way."

Silver was lying at their feet where he would be in line for any scraps. He knew that Chris was generous and usually shared with him. After they finished eating, the dog knew he had received all that was coming his way so he got up for a splash in the river, but he came out shortly and started to growl while looking back down the trail in the direction from which they had come.

Glory started to whinny and step around in a nervous manner. Brian jumped up and caught her bridle and put his hand on her neck, then said quietly but sternly and with urgency in his voice, "Jennifer, you and Chris get on your horses quickly and start riding up the trail." As Jennifer jumped up he said, "Now don't panic. I don't want you to startle the horses, but hurry."

When Jennifer and Chris were both mounted and had their horses moving, Jennifer, who was terrified, asked in a shaking voice, "What is it?"

Brian, who was just swinging his leg over Glory's back, said, "There is a bear coming up behind; Chris, call Silver to

53

go with you. I don't want him tackling this fellow. He looks big and mean."

Jennifer wanted to tell Chris to hurry up and move so she could gallop away like it's done in the movies, without realizing it took a lot more riding skill than she possessed to stay on the back of a running horse. But she couldn't get her voice to work as her vocal cords were seized with fear. She hoped it wasn't a grizzly; she had heard about them, how they will attack people for no reason, and wondered how safe they were on the horses. Then she remembered Brian's gun and was glad for the first time that he had brought it, after all.

As Brian rode off behind Chris and Jennifer, the bear came into full view from the shrub and started sniffing around where they had eaten their lunch. He picked up a crust of bread that Silver had missed, ate it, and looked around for more. Seeing that it was food the bear was looking for, Brian called out, "Jennifer, if you have any more of those apples, you had better get rid of them. They can smell them a mile away, and that's probably what he's after."

With hands cold and stiff from fear, Jennifer reached for her saddle bag and tried to untie the flap as Brian rode up beside her. "Can you manage, or should I help you?"

"I can manage, thanks. I guess I shouldn't have brought apples." But she couldn't untie the flap because of her shaking hands, so Brian had to do it. She tried to read his thoughts while he was undoing the flap, but he kept his eyes cast on what he was doing and all she could see was the inscrutable Logan mask on his face, "I'm sorry I didn't know." She was feeling perplexed as she dropped the apples on the ground when Brian finally got the flap undone as it was difficult from the angle of his horse. She saw his face tighten so knew he was controlling himself when he spoke.

"Don't worry. I never thought of it earlier when I saw you bring them out." Looking at the apples on the ground he said, "That should keep him busy for a while. Now let's get away from here." Brian rode up to the front to set the pace, but kept looking back to see if the bear was following them. He recalled how Jennifer had been terrified when he said there was a bear.

He felt sure that she would have tried to get her horse to run and would have ended upon the ground if Chris hadn't been in her way. He wondered at his wisdom in letting her come, and knew she had to learn their way of life sometime; she wouldn't be happy staying at home by herself. When they had traveled for a while, Brian said, "I think we can relax now. I don't think Mr. Bear is coming this far."

"Maybe he's still eating the apples. I hope he gets a stomach ache." Chris was giggling at the thought.

Jennifer was feeling like a fool, but she was also shaking like a leaf. I was scared to death, she thought, scared to death of a bear that only wanted some food, a bear that even a little boy can joke about. But it's the first one I ever saw that wasn't enclosed in Stanley Park in Vancouver, and they look a lot different outside. I'll never get used to it, I guess.

The afternoon sun was warm and they were all a bit drowsy from their lunch so they rode in silence, while Silver skirted the shrub on either side looking for something to chase. The pace of the horses was too slow for him after the excitement of the bear, and he wanted a wild rabbit or a squirrel to have some fun with, but none could be found, so he gave up and followed along at Jingle's heels behind Chris.

6   Trouble on the Trail

They entered a stand of poplars that were a mass of yellow leaves all falling to the ground, like a curtain coming down, Jennifer thought wearily. The splendor of the sight was like the curtain in Vancouver's Queen Elizabeth Theatre, where they would be rehearsing for the first opera of the season. But the curtain could be going up, not down. She wondered what they would be presenting this year, with a little pang in her heart. She had enjoyed doing *Carmen*, *La Traviata*, and *Madame Butterfly* the year before. It had been a happy year at the theatre while planning her wedding to Brian when the season ended. She didn't think she would miss it; there seemed to be so many more wonderful things to look forward to, to take its place. She had been the envy of all the girls, not to mention the guys, in the chorus, going to live on a ranch in the interior of B.C., with horses to ride and all that fresh air to breathe.

Before she had come to live at Windsong, she had planned on giving piano and voice lessons. But there was already a teacher in Golden who handled all the pupils who wanted lessons; so she got a job working in the supermarket. She would be singing for the people at all the local weddings when they got to know her better, she expected. That is, if they ever got over their resentment of her. Some of the people made her feel as if they blamed her for Joanne's death. She wasn't sure, but she could feel a resentment of some kind. It was obvious that everyone in the whole town and the surrounding area had loved Joanne. She had taken an active part in all the goings on in the community, and had been a very capable person. People spoke of her as they would of a saint. Joanne hadn't been a native either, but being a dedicated school teacher she got to know people very quickly and became a part of the community. This made it even harder for Jennifer. She felt as if she was in competition with a ghost, and she didn't want to feel that way. Brian said it was just the small town way, and not to worry; it would take time to break the ice.

Once, when she was particularly upset about a remark that someone had made in the store, Brian offered to look for a teaching position at the coast and take her back there where she might be happier, and she could return to singing with the opera. But she had convinced him that she loved living at Windsong. This was where she would have to raise their family.

The people of Golden were just going to have to put up with her the way she was, and she also would learn to accept them. She was firm in her decision at the time, but with the change in Christopher's and Brian's attitudes she wondered if she was ever going to belong here. Since she had fallen in love with Brian, her life hadn't been easy. First there was the trouble with Gail which she still found hard to understand, especially when it was Gail who introduced them in the first place. She went through periods of wondering whether Brian really loved her or if he had married her to get a mother for Chris and a house-keeper. He had been good to her; she couldn't complain about that, but he spent a lot of time with Chris, and when he wasn't doing things with him, he was worrying about him for one reason or another.

She hadn't expected that. What had she expected? she wondered. To be loved and cherished? She had her own ideas of what marriage would be like. If she couldn't be number one, at least she wanted to be on par with Chris. She was a realist, she thought, and hadn't expected a bed of roses, but she must have anticipated it to have a bit of a rosy glow, which it didn't seem to have of late.

Now she had no way of knowing what could be expected of their marriage.

She looked up at the pale blue autumn sky that could be seen through the partially undressed branches of the poplar trees, and heard the rustle of the withered leaves under the horses' hooves. She suddenly became overwhelmed by the immensity of the preparations taking place around her for the coming winter, when all that was now surrounding her would be covered with snow. She wondered what winter in this part of the country must be like to require such total consideration on the part of both animals and plants. Nature planned well and rarely exaggerated, of that she was sure.

A touch of anxiety seeped in at the thought that she too must endure a winter like none she had ever known. She thought of Vancouver with its rain and fog, and the odd bit of snow. But the lawns stayed green all year. She had gone up Grouse Mountain and Seymour to ski when she was young. When she was older she drove up Howe Sound to the great ski realm of Whistler. But her winter experience was limited to the ski slopes, and not to the roads and highways. She was a little apprehensive about driving in ice and snow in extremely low temperatures, like the ones she heard they sometimes have in Golden.

Brian loved the feeling of well being the mountains gave him. The power he felt there restored his strength and replenished his soul. His son was an offshoot of this soil, and he had a natural gift for understanding the habits of the animals and the reason for the changing of the forests during the four seasons. He remembered how Joanne had been a lover of natural things, always aware of any unusual rock formation or growth to display in her classroom for her pupils to see. She had adopted the way of life at Windsong, the way animals and fowl of the wilds have, over the centuries, by coloring themselves with shades that blend with the rocks and shrubs they inhabit. The browns of the grouse, the fawn of the deer, and the varying shades of gray-brown of the Rocky Mountain sheep while the stone sheep further north are white, because their habitat is covered with snow. Therefore, Brian was unconsciously watching Jennifer, feeling she was disappointed in this way of life, and that maybe they both had made a mistake

Chris looked back and saw that Jennifer was lagging behind again. He was becoming impatient to see Sam, not having seen him since the day before when he left for school. He felt that it was Jennifer's fault that they couldn't catch up to him, because she just rode along as slow as she could, and he thought maybe she didn't want to find Sam. She did things that she didn't like doing to please his father, he knew, and if that was why she was coming along, the sooner he got rid of her the better. He said, "Can't you ride faster, Jennifer? We are never going to catch up to Sam if you don't hurry."

"I'm going as fast as I can."

"Then maybe you should go home so Dad and I can catch up to Sam."

The tone of voice he had suddenly used when Brian was ahead of them and out of earshot annoyed her, so without thinking she spoke angrily. "Sam, Sam, Sam, that's all you think about. I'm getting tired of hearing about that stupid sheep."

"Mommy loves him, even if you don't," he said as he spurred his horse and caught up to Brian, with resentment at her words against Sam smoldering inside. Jennifer regretted her outburst, as her words had made Chris compare her to his mother in defence of his love for Sam.

They came out of the poplars and Brian pulled up his horse. Chris stopped behind him and as Jennifer pulled up she said, "You know, for a minute I thought I heard a train whistle." Brian smiled and said, "You did." The train whistled again, and the sound was loud and clear; there was no mistaking it, as it echoed through the mountains. Jennifer had a bewildered look on her face, so Brian reminded her that they had been following the Kicking Horse River that ran through the Kicking Horse Pass and so did the railroad, and the Trans-Canada Highway for that matter, and they were both down below them not very far away.

"And I thought we were off in the wilderness some place,

and here we are right next to civilization all the time," she said with the sound of relief showing in her voice.

"Well, don't worry about it," Brian said, "It looks like we are going into the wilderness right now, because Sam seems to be heading that way."

"How do you know, Dad?" Chris asked. "You didn't get off and check for tracks, so how do you know where he's going? Maybe we have lost him." Chris was getting upset. "We are going too slow to catch Sam, that's what the trouble is," he said, giving Jennifer a look of resentment. Brian became very concerned at the intensity of Christopher's outburst. He had forgotten about his son's seriousness over tracking Sam and had been enjoying the ride on such a made-to-order fall day. He stepped over to Christopher's pony and looked up into his son's face, so like his own, but for a fleeting moment it was much like his mother's. Brian's heart turned over. His annoyance at Chris for having spoiled his happy feeling vanished and he spoke in a softer tone. "Look, Chris, Silver is following Sam; that's why he is turning up Dark Creek and wants us to follow. I don't think Sam is going along the Kicking Horse any more." Silver was sniffing and barking and running back and forth. He was getting excited because no one was following his lead. "Okay, Silver, we're coming." Brian turned to Jennifer, "Let's just follow along up Dark Creek for a few minutes so he knows we got the message and stops barking, then we can stop for a rest."

Brian noticed the strained look on Jennifer's face and he thought, damn, she is going to spoil the whole trip for us, having to stop all the time to rest. She could have put a little more effort into learning how to ride when she decided to come along. He had warned her what it would be like, but she had insisted on going anyway, saying she would manage just fine.

"Have we got anything we can snack on since we got rid of the apples?"

"Oh, I think I might be able to find something without you having to hunt us a bear." Jennifer was so relieved that they were going to stop for a while that she had said the first thing that came into her mind, but retracted it immediately. "I didn't mean that." She was still unnerved by her outburst at Chris.

But Brian had already started to laugh, so Chris laughed too. They knew she had been scared to death when they saw the bear; so Brian said in his most teasing tone of voice, "Guess we better find a bear for Mom."

"Yeah," Chris laughed sarcastically, "so she can make some bear sandwiches."

They were both still chuckling at her confusion when after turning up Dark Creek behind Silver they stopped and dismounted for a welcome respite, so she said, "All right, you guys, if you don't stop laughing I won't give you any cookies." She brought out the cookie container and sat on a log between Brian and Chris. When she removed the cover, a strong aroma of peanut butter assailed their nostrils, and they both reached for cookies at the same time and their hands clashed above the container. Then it was Jennifer's turn to laugh, but it was a nervous one as she still felt foolish over the ribbing they had given her when she inadvertently mentioned the bear. "All right, boys," she said, "now mind your manners, one at a time." They all munched noisily away on the crisp cookies, and after their deserved reprimand from Jennifer, Brian and Chris remembered to thank her for making their favorite ones which were being thoroughly enjoyed. Even Silver had caught the scent and come to beg a few crumbs.

Brian had a good sense of humor. He had enjoyed many a good laugh when hearing of the pranks played on dudes visiting the ranches around Golden. The pranks usually involved some greenhorn who thought there was nothing to mastering the art of riding a horse. They seemed to think that if the locals could do it, they could do it. And as a result the dudes usually ended up walking bow-legged the next day and carrying a cushion to sit on. Brian was reminded of this when he saw Jennifer sit gingerly down on the log. He was amused, and was about to chide her about it. But when he looked at the determined set of her jaw, he knew there was no way she was going to admit to it; so he said nothing, but he had to admire her grit.

"When are we likely to get our first fall of snow?" Jennifer asked, dreading the thought. She looked around where they were having their rest, and pictured it with snow, and hoped it

61

would be impossible to ride horses in the winter. She then recalled having seen two snowmobiles in one of the sheds at Windsong, and wondered if they came up here on them. Her one consolation of the dreaded winter had been that they couldn't go up into the hills.

"It could snow anytime after Indian summer is over," Brian told her. "Some years we don't get much snow before Christmas, just depends on what kind of winter we have."

"Do you use the snowmobiles much? Do you come up here with them?"

"We use them to get out to North Bench Road when the road to the ranch drifts in and yes, on weekends, sometimes we ride up into the hills."

"Sounds like fun," she lied, while a feeling of absolute dread came over her.

"Do you think you could drive one?" Brian suddenly realized that Jennifer would be going to work after he and Chris left for school.

"I can learn," she said skeptically. "By the way, a Greg Logan was in the store on Friday and said to say hello."

"I haven't seen Greg in years."

"Thinking of winter reminded me; he said to stop and say hello when we go skiing in the Bugaboos. When do you think we will go?"

"Around the end of January or February is the best time, there is lots of snow by then."

"Dad goes every year, and I get to stay at Grandma's, don't you, Dad? But I can go to Lake Louise when he goes there, it's not too steep for me."

Jennifer was glad to hear that Chris couldn't go to the Bugaboos. She would have Brian to herself for a while. With the thought of skiing her fear of winter in this wild country abated some, until Brian spoke again.

"Do you think you can ski well enough for heli-skiing? They fly you up to the lodge and then up to the slope the next day. It's for advanced skiers. There are no lifts, they take you up by helicopter and you do 10,000 vertical feet in two trips."

"There you go again, thinking I can't do anything when you

already said we would go." But she didn't feel as confident as she sounded, as heli-skiing from what Brian had just said sounded more difficult than she had thought. But she was going anyway, so she could have Brian to herself for a few days away from Chris.

"Okay, okay," he said.

But she wondered why it is when you couldn't hear, people think you didn't understand, and when you are in unfamiliar circumstances they think you don't have what it takes to cope. What ever happened to hearing and learning?

Their conversation was interrupted by Silver, whom they hadn't notice wander off. He came running out of the bush followed by a coyote. The instant the coyote saw the spectators he reversed his direction in a flash, as did Silver, then it was Silver chasing the coyote. It was an unbelievably comical sight to behold. The three Logans laughed until they couldn't laugh any more.

Christopher sighed in resignation. He wanted desperately to catch up to Sam and they seemed to be stopping all the time for one reason or another, and now it was Silver, whom he adored, that was holding them up while he chased the coyote.

"Now we'll have to wait for Silver to come back. I hope he doesn't chase that coyote all day. I want to catch up to Sam pretty soon, don't you, Dad?"

"We'll catch up to him, don't worry. I'm a little surprised he took this turn and I'm getting really curious about where he's going."

"Where are we anyway? What direction are we going, I'm all turned around." Jennifer was reluctant to ask, not wanting Brian to be able to discredit her again, but she wanted to get her bearings.

"We were going east along the Kicking Horse, but now it looks like we going to be following Dark Creek, and it runs in a north easterly direction to the South Fork of Hospital Creek, which runs down the valley by Table Mountain. That's Lookout Mountain over there across the pass." Brian was a good teacher, and liked explaining things. Jennifer looked in the direction Brian was pointing and caught sight of something glimmering in the sun.

"It doesn't look like the highest mountain to put a lookout on. Is that what's glittering in the sun?"

"Yes. It's not the highest mountain, but it's accessible, and you can see all over from up there. I rode Glory up there a couple of summers ago; there's a pretty good trail, a four wheel drive would make it. There's an old trail along Dark Creek, too, so we will have easy going as long as Sam follows the creek."

"Are we still on the west side of the divide?" Jennifer asked, as she was determined to learn all she could about the interior of British Columbia, especially the East Kootenay region around Golden where she expected to be spending the rest of her life. She hadn't even heard of Golden until she met Gail Forbes at college, and she told her about going to visit her sister and brother-in-law who lived on a ranch. She hadn't even known that Yoho National Park was in B.C. until she saw a picture of a beautiful lake that Brian had, and he said it was Emerald Lake and consequently she had learned that it was in Yoho National Park. She got excited thinking of all the beautiful and historical things there must be to see living so close to three national parks.

"I don't think we will be going as far as the Divide, Jennifer. It is on the B.C. - Alberta border." Brian was beginning to be annoyed again by her ignorance, so she decided not to ask any more questions for a while.

Silver returned, and Brian said, "Okay, time to get going, rest's over." But when Jennifer got on her horse, it didn't seem like she wanted to move. She nudged her a bit with her heel as she saw Brian and Chris do, but not too hard because she didn't want to hurt her. When the horse still wouldn't go, Jennifer slapped her gently on the neck with the reins and said, "Come on, Bess, get up," but the mare just took a few more steps and stopped. Brian and Chris were already moving along the trail, and she started to get a bit panicky about being left behind, so she called to Brian, "I think Bess is getting tired."

Brian stopped his horse and turned around to see what was going on. It only took him one minute to size up the situation.

He had purchased Bess for Jennifer after they were married. He still had Bell at the ranch, as Chris didn't want him to get rid of her because she had been his mother's horse. But he didn't feel that Jennifer could handle a high spirited horse like Bell, so he bought Bess from a neighbor. She was a gentle mare and easy to handle. But she was no fool, it seemed, as she had learned that Jennifer was a softie and would let her have her way. He turned his horse around and rode back and gave Bess a swat on the rump that made her take off lively up the trail, and Jennifer had to grab the saddle horn in fear and to keep from falling off.

"You have got to be firm with her, or she is going to rule you and do as she pleases." His previous annoyance, which had bothered her, had been mild compared to the disgust his voice now held, and brought Jennifer close to tears. "Well, I don't want to be mean to her."

"You don't have to be mean, just be firm, that's all." He was completely exasperated with her. Christopher was having a good laugh at Jennifer's expense for the second time that day.

She wished she had learned to ride a horse when she was young, instead of learning to play Mozart on the piano and reach high C for Mr. Hugo Smalz, her voice teacher.

The riding was easier along Dark Creek, as they found the old road that was just a rugged trail in Jennifer's opinion, but she supposed a four wheel drive could travel on it like Brian said, but she wouldn't be fussy about being one of the occupants. You would be in for a lot of bumping and jarring. It was almost enjoyable riding along in the afternoon sunshine with the sound of the creek rushing beside them.

Jennifer noticed that she didn't find the smell of the horses' sweaty bodies offensive as she had before, and she liked the smell of the leather saddles, but she was getting tired. She felt grubby and dirty and longed for a refreshing shower. She looked at the creek but knew she didn't dare suggest stopping, so she could soak her feet which were aching badly in the unfamiliar riding boots, and wash some of the sweat and grime from her face. With her growing discomfort her annoyance at Chris for wanting to follow the sheep returned in greater intensity, but after the episode with the bear she wouldn't even consider going back home alone.

They came to a bright sunny area along the creek where all the trees were about same height. Jennifer asked about the uniformity of the trees and the absence of giant timber, and Brian told her that a fire had destroyed all the trees and they had been replanted by the forest service. The road was clear of logs and debris, so they got off and walked for a while, leading their horses.

After walking only a short way, Jennifer's feet that were already sore from the hardness of the leather riding boots became more painful than she could bear; so heedless of their wrath, she announced, "I'm going to stop and soak my feet for a few minutes in the creek. They are killing me."

Brian resignedly held the reins of her horse, not wanting to take a chance on Bess starting for home again, while Jennifer took off her boots and socks at the edge of the creek and plunged her aching feet into the water. Relief was almost instant, so cold was the water in Dark Creek at that time of year. So after a very few minutes she was ready to put on her boots and be on her way. But after she had her boots on, she couldn't resist stepping on the wet stones at the edge of the creek, and splashing some of the refreshing water onto her burning face. The rocks were slippery and gave no traction to the leather soles of her riding boots, and as she bent to cup some water in her hands, she fell into the icy waters of the creek. She came out dripping wet, shivering with cold, and humiliated to the point of tears, to face Brian and Chris who stood there with looks of incredulity on their faces. No one spoke, while Jennifer shivered, but Brian went to the pack horse to get her pack so she could change her clothes, while Chris, who was so angry at the further delay he couldn't utter a word, rode on ahead by himself. For the first time in Jennifer's life she had to change her clothes without the privacy of her own room, and suddenly found herself reluctant to do so. Brian, sensing her modesty, said, "Oh for God's sake, Jennifer, who do you think is watching?" And Jennifer, who had imagined eyes peering at her from behind every bush, became more self-conscious than ever, and felt even the leaves on the trees were watching her.

When she was dressed again in appropriate riding clothes and her wet pants and shirt were draped over the packs on Nelliebell to dry, she and Brian mounted up and followed Chris. As Chris rode on ahead up the logging road after Jennifer had fallen into the creek, his disappointment in her occupied his mind for a time.

She was totally unsuitable as his mother, he decided, because she couldn't ride, or do anything else like Mommy had, it seemed. Then that day he kept buried deep inside, and tried not to think about, forced itself into his mind. It was the worst day of his life. It was worse than the days when Mommy had cried a lot, and he had tried to play quietly and not upset her further, but when Dad came home she couldn't even tell him why she was crying. Chris had gone to bed on those nights upset and confused, but in the morning she was usually her wonderful self again. It hadn't been like that on the awful day, and the memory of it filled him with intolerable pain. He woke that morning with a feeling of impending doom. It was summer and the sun was shining through his bedroom window, and yet it seemed dark and cold in the room. He couldn't hear any sound of movement in the house, so he got up and went into the kitchen looking for his mother, but there was no-one there. "Mommy," he called, several times, but there was no answer.

He heard the washing machine going in the basement, so he went down the stairs to find her sorting clothes. She was startled when she looked up and saw him there. She had a strained look on her face that frightened him.

"Chris," she said. "Do you want some breakfast?" When he didn't reply she put down the clothes she was holding and said, "I'll go up and make you an egg."

"I'm not hungry," he said, as the odor from the steam and detergent filled his nostrils and repelled him.

"You must have something." And she moved toward the stairs instead of taking him in her arms and giving him a morning kiss like she usually did.

"No, I'm not hungry, I feel sick."

"Well, go back to bed, then," she said with indifference, and went back to sorting clothes.

He wasn't sick, but he went back to bed and lay there weighted down with the pressure of something terrible about to happen. He watched a big fly that had found its way into the house crawl across the ceiling. It flew to the window, and he thought of getting up and trying to catch it, but he didn't move from the bed.

Mommy seemed preoccupied when she came and got him up for lunch. She didn't talk to him, so he was quiet too, while she made him a sandwich that he only nibbled at because he still couldn't eat. Then she said that she was taking him to Auntie Cheryl's, but she stopped at the store on the way and bought him a big package of gum. She had never let him have that much gum all at once before, and it confused him, so he just sat and looked at it in his hand without opening it.

Aunt Cheryl opened the door with a smile of welcome that faded to a look of concern as she saw the stress on her sister-in-law's face. She reached out to her and said, "Come in and have a cup of coffee."

"No, no, I can't, I have to go," Joanne said as she put her arms around Chris and covered his face with kisses. Then she ran down the steps and out to her car.

Chris was seized with an unknown fear as he heard the engine roar into action and he started to run after his mother, apprehension mounting. He was stopped by his aunt, who said, "Come and see the new baby kittens." But the sight of his mother's car disappearing down the road in a cloud of dust was imprinted on his mind forever.

The next thing Chris could recall of that day was when his father came to pick him up. His father was crying and when he talked to Aunt Cheryl, she cried too. They phoned Grandpa Forbes in Vancouver, and all the relatives came to Golden. But nothing was explained to Chris, and when he asked questions he was given ambiguous answers with a false brightness that did nothing to help him understand what had happened, so he stopped asking and remained engulfed in a wall of silence that bewildered and frightened him. On the day of the funeral, Chris was left at the Wilson's house along with their two children and a babysitter. Mr. Wilson was a friend of his father's, and they taught at the same school, but Chris didn't like Marty or Jenny Wilson much as they were town kids and didn't know anything about animals or living on a ranch.

Besides which, they had lived in Victoria on Vancouver Island before their father accepted a teaching position in Golden, and Chris felt that they thought they were just a little bit better than he was. They were always talking about Victoria as if it was better than Golden and that annoyed him, so he wasn't happy about having to stay there that afternoon. He didn't feel like playing with anyone. His stomach hurt and he felt like crying, as he didn't understand what had happened to Mommy.

When his father came to pick him up and take him to Grandma Logan's house, Chris was happy, but when he saw all the cars that were parked outside he was disappointed, so he sidled in around the door and peered into the living room, hoping to find his mother there. He was greeted by the staring faces of strangers with red, swollen eyes and puffy faces, and his heart sank to the pit of his stomach. He felt like he was going to be sick. Then his Grandma Forbes came and took him in her arms and kissed him, and called him "her darling," and it made him feel better for a time.

His grandmother led him to the kitchen away from the staring faces. There was food everywhere and she offered Chris some, but he refused. When she coaxed him he accepted a plate, but he didn't touch it. He just sat there staring at the potato salad, and ham, and turkey, and all the things he loved to eat, while his stomach churned inside him and his mind became more and more confused. His father came in and sat beside him and gathered him into his arms and onto his lap. His eyes were all red and puffy too, and Chris felt more lost and bewildered than ever. "Where is Mommy?" he cried.

"Chris," his father said, and stopped. "Chris, Mommy's gone to heaven, so you and I will have to look after each other." And he stopped again, unable to say any more.

No one mentioned Mommy in the days that followed. It was as if they were not allowed to talk about her, or so it seemed to

Chris. The relatives all went home, leaving Brian and Chris alone at Windsong for the remainder of the summer.

Chris was a very lonely little boy who cried himself to sleep every night. He could still see Mommy leaving in the car that awful day and he wished with all his heart that he had run after her and stopped her. And now again so deep was his anguish that he cried out unaware of what he was doing, as he had many times in the interim of her leaving, "I shouldn't have let her go." But only the stillness of the wilderness, broken by the gurgling of the creek, heard his cry. A desolate loneliness engulfed him and smote his heart.

Chris didn't know that his mother wasn't coming back. Nobody had explained to him that it was final, so in his lonely bed at night he started thinking that maybe heaven was a hospital where she had gone, like the other times, but further away and that was why they couldn't go and see her, but she would come back. So he started making plans for her return. First he would tell her how sorry he was for being bad, and promise to never be bad again if she wouldn't go away to the hospital any more, as he missed her when she was gone. Then they would do things together like they had before. They would go riding in the meadow and racing around the pond. He would win sometimes now that he was bigger. He had won before when racing with Mommy, but he suspected that she had let him win when he saw her hands on the reins holding Bell in check. By the time winter came, he would be big enough to sit in front on the toboggan and hold the rope to steer.

When winter came and the snow piled up they could go out after dinner when the moon was bright, and coast down the hill to the pond. He could help Dad even better now to clear the snow from the pond and build a big bonfire. Mommy would bring hot dogs for roasting. He had a new knife in his pocket that Dad had given him as a reward for cleaning up the yard so he could sharpen up the sticks just like Dad did. It was his plans for his mother's return that had kept him from despair in the days that followed that awful day she went away. Thinking of his plans again made him excited, so he nudged Jingle in the flank with his heel to make him go faster as his need to catch up with Sam became more urgent.

Chris was jarred from his thoughts by the shying of his horse. He saw something move in the bush at the side of the road. Thinking it was only a bear or some other harmless animal he was not frightened, until a figure jumped out onto the road in front of Jingle and the pony reared up, nearly throwing Chris to the ground. Then, the figure that looked like a man in dirty old clothes grabbed Jingle's bridle, and the pony started to snort and skitter nervously backwards down the road.

"Let go!" Chris yelled.

But the man just laughed and said, "You get off now."

"You let go of my horse," Chris demanded in his toughest voice, while his heart started pounding in his chest.

But the man just laughed harder and said, "You're funny. It's my horse now, kid. Teach you to ride out here alone, eh? Now get off."

The attacker reeked with sweat and alcohol, and as Chris noticed that he was slurring his words like he was drunk, the boy became more frightened than ever. This was a situation that he had never encountered before, and he wasn't sure how he should handle it. But Brian, who had heard Chris yell, had spurred Glory to a gallop and was on the scene behind Chris in a matter of minutes.

"Hey, you," Brian yelled, "Let go of that horse."

At that moment Chris took his reins and lashed at the man, striking him across the shoulders. This only angered him and he grabbed tighter on the bridle and started cursing Chris as he reached to pull the boy from the saddle, but the horse started pawing the ground as the bit cut cruelly into his mouth, and he raked his hoof across the man's foot. This angered the attacker further and he turned his wrath on Chris by screaming out, "You dirty little bastard, get off!"

Brian recognized the intruder as a biker by the death head club colors on the back of his ragged, denim vest, and knew that he probably wasn't alone. How many, he wondered. And then, just as he was about to ride up beside Chris to corner the man between them so he could give the guy what he had coming, he

71

saw another figure emerge from the bush on the other side of him, and this one looked even meaner than the first.

"Come on, old man," he slurred. "We just want to have a ride on your horses, and you can have a ride on our bikes." And he pointed to the bikes parked in the trees.

"Just a friendly little exchange, nothing to get excited about." And he laughed an ugly, leering laugh.

As Brian looked where the man was pointing he saw three bikes half hidden by the bush, and knew that there was yet a third member of this group to be reckoned with. The odds were even worse than it had appeared. At that moment Jennifer rode around the bend and saw what was going on ahead. She screamed, and as Brian turned to instruct Jennifer to ride up beside him he saw that the third man was already approaching Jennifer's horse. He was a husky brute in dirty, black leather biker's garb and his long hair stuck out in a filthy tangled mass.

"Hey, a woman," the second one on the road said as he started moving in her direction as well. "We'll take her instead of the horses, fellas, come on." Jennifer became absolutely terrified when she saw the two filthy bikers approaching her with their ugly grinning mouths and yellow teeth. She was about to wheel her horse around and start riding back down the trail when Brian, who had read her thoughts, called, "Sit tight, Jennifer," and he manoeuvred Glory to the side of the road where he could watch all three men. "Stop right where you are!" he commanded.

But the two who were after Jennifer just laughed and kept on walking in her direction.

"Just what we need for the night you guys, a woman to keep us company. Come on, Julian." The second one with the dirty red plaid shirt called to the one who was still trying to grab the reins from Chris as the boy swung them repeatedly, lashing his attacker wherever the reins struck, turning him into an enraged beast.

"By God I'll have you too, you little rat. I like blond hair and blue eyes."

"Oh come on, Julian, let's get the woman, she's better, brown eyes I like."

And he laughed in an ugly, suggestive way. "Look, she's clean, too," he said as he noticed Jennifer's wet hair from her fall in the creek. "Been skinny dipping in the creek, I'll bet." He leered, as he continued to stagger towards Jennifer, who was lashing her reins at the big burly brute who was nearing her horse, as she had seen Chris doing.

Brian was furious when he heard the ugly threats being made to Chris and Jennifer. No scum like this was going to talk to his wife and son like that, and yet he knew he had to keep his cool. He also knew that no reasonable means was going to stop these drunken fools, so he reached for his gun on the side of the saddle. "Stop right there," he ordered in the cool, controlled voice of a person driven to desperate measures.

The tone of Brian's command stopped all three men in their tracks. They hadn't noticed the gun on the side of Brian's saddle, so intent were they upon Chris and Jennifer, but they now saw the rifle cradled in Brian's arms and froze in their tracks.

"We didn't mean any harm," the one called Julian said, as he stepped away from Christopher's horse. "We were just having a little fun. We weren't going to hurt anyone, were we, guys?" "No," the other two chorused in shaking voices.

Brian's anger showed in his voice as he turned to the two who had been harassing Jennifer, as he said, "Get away from her."

As the two men stepped back Jennifer rode her horse up beside Brian, and the man accosting Chris moved over to the side of the road with his two companions.

"Now get on your damn bikes and get the hell out of here before I lose my temper, and don't let me set eyes on any of you round here again!" Brian said, and the bikers hastened to obey. They were gathering their belongings from the bush and packing them on their bikes when Silver, who had been off in the bush tracking a coyote during the entire episode, returned. Brian heard him snarl and commanded him to stay, just as he was about to leap on the back of one of the bikers and tear him to shreds. This hastened their departure, and they jumped onto their bikes which they started with a roar that set all three horses to a nervous prancing despite the tight rein that both Brian and Chris held on them. Brian had instinctively grabbed the bridle on Jennifer's horse to steady her. Then they rode off down the logging road bouncing over the rough terrain without a backward glance.

"Are they gone, Dad?" Chris asked. "I'd say they are," Brian said. "Can't hear their bikes any more, so they must be miles away..."

"But they might come back," Jennifer said in a shaking voice.

"I don't think so," Brian said. "No, they won't be back, not after Silver arrived on the scene. He stopped any ideas they might have had of returning to surprise us. I think they were just a bunch of drunken cowards with enough sense left to get out of a losing situation."

"They won't be back because they're scared of Dad's gun, too. You'd use it wouldn't you, Dad, if you had to."

"Would you have?" Jennifer asked. She was thankful for a second time that day that Brian had brought the gun. They had their place after all, but the thought of using it against humans unnerved her, so she added, "Against human beings?"

"You call those human beings?" Brian intoned. "Why, they are nothing but filthy animals, and that's an insult to the animals. Poor fools, wasting their lives on alcohol and drugs. But to answer your question, if they had touched either one of you, I would have fired into the air and I'm sure that would have been enough to send them packing. I'm glad it didn't get that far, as Jennifer's horse would have bolted, throwing her, because she doesn't hold the reins tight enough."

I'm always at fault, Jennifer thought.

Chris had more important things on his mind than drunken bikers. It was just another incident along the way, although a bit more unusual than most, and something to talk about when he got back to school, but nothing to deter him from his purpose, so he said, "Let's get going, we've got to find Sam."

Jennifer took several nervous looks down the trail, and then moved her horse to the side of the road so that Brian could pass. She saw his grin.

"I'll ride rear for a bit, and Chris can lead," Brian said, and then added when he saw the pleased look on Christopher's face, "Set us a good pace for a while so we can leave this unfortunate incident behind us."

Jennifer felt safer riding in the middle, even having Chris on one side of her made her feel better, as he seemed to know how to handle himself in any situation in this dangerous wild country. She had expected the threat of wild animals, but to encounter wild men under the influence of liquor and drugs was the farthest thing from her mind. She liked having Brian riding behind her, it brought him closer to her. Then she realized that he was in a position to observe her every error in handling a horse. So be it, she thought, and rode on.

"Where do you think those degenerates came from?" Jennifer half turned in her saddle to ask Brian, and in so doing she tightened the reins, so Bess stopped.

"Keep going," Brian said with a slight irritation in his voice, and then in a more natural tone, "Probably from Calgary. That's one of the dangers of being so close to the Trans-Canada Highway, they ride through Golden in the summer in gangs. They seem to like racing up in the Rogers Pass where the highway is smooth and wide, and camping in the wilderness up there where they can party all night without being disturbed. A gang of them stopped in Golden last summer by the river, but the R.C.M.P. told them to hit the road."

"They come from the cities," Chris said triumphantly. I'll bet there are lots of bikers in Vancouver and Victoria, too."

"There are some in Vancouver," Jennifer admitted, "but not in Kerrisdale." Brian laughed. "I'll bet," he said in a voice that suggested that he knew better.

"Oh, let's forget about them," Chris said. "Let's just hurry so we can catch up to Sam. I sure hope those bikers didn't scare him off. Do you think they did, Dad?" he asked anxiously, as the fear that Sam may have run off somewhere instead of leading them to his destination entered his mind.

"No, Silver is still following his tracks," Brian said with more assurance than he felt, because the thought that the sheep may have run off headlong into the bush when the bikes roared down the road had crossed Brian's mind as well. Encouraged by his father's words, Chris set an even faster pace than before.

Jennifer was awed by the vastness of the area that the fire had destroyed, and the enormous project it must have been to replant the trees. Brian said it had been some years before, and that his Grandfather had told him stories when he was young of forest fires that covered the area with a thick cloud of smoke that hung over the valley for days, when they could hardly see the sun, and they sweltered in the heat under a sun they couldn't see, in an eerie light, and at night the whole sky was red from the reflection of the fire. The Columbia River Lumber Co., one of the largest holders of standing timber in B.C., had to shut down because a fire destroyed their timber.

Brian's father told him when he was a little boy he had been afraid to go to sleep at night when there was a forest fire in the mountains in case it came and burned their house, after listening to the old stories. Jennifer wanted to know if there was any danger of fire at Windsong, and Brian said there was always some danger in a dry year, but there weren't any large stands of timber around Windsong, and the yard and pastures were clear, so there was no danger to the house. She was becoming more conscious of the forces of nature since moving to Golden. The potential that it possessed to create both splendor and havoc was staggering.

They rode along in the afternoon sun that contained the heat of a summer day for a few short hours. They even took some pictures with the movie camera, and scanned the terrain with the binoculars. They saw a bull moose making his way upstream on Dark Creek, but knew he would be long gone before they reached that point. They remarked that he would have made a nice picture. But they saw no sign of their own precious wild animal, as they had come to consider Sam in the years he had lived at the ranch. Chris became upset again, as he did every time they looked for Sam and couldn't see him. Brian assured him again and again that they were on Sam's trail, and that they would catch up to him in due time.

It had been a long day for Jennifer. She ached all over, and her rear end (as she called it) was so sore she couldn't sit down.

She wondered if it was possible to get a buttock blister. If so, she had blisters a mile high, she was sure. She had hoped all day that they would find where the sheep went and be able to return home by night, but now she knew they were destined to spend the night in that awful little tent, and shuddered at the thought of the three of them sleeping in such close quarters. For the first time that day she wished she had stayed home.

The sun's rays were beginning to slant and the air had a coolness again, so they dismounted and put on their jackets. Jennifer was scanning the side of the creek for a suitable place to spend the night. She thought she saw several but didn't want to be the one to mention stopping, fearing a rebuff from Chris, so she dragged on leaving the decision up to Brian. But it didn't look like he was giving it any thought. She was close to becoming completely exhausted and knew she couldn't climb back on that horse if she had to, and it looked like she had to, as Brian was back on Glory and Chris had mounted Jingle.

Then to her great relief she heard Brian say, "I think if we ride a bit longer we can reach a little cabin by Hospital Creek." Jennifer's heart lifted at the thought of a cabin instead of the tent for the night, but Brian continued, "It would be handy to store our gear in as the weather can change in a flash. You can't trust it." He didn't add it would be a good place to store their food in case a bear came snooping round.

"Can't we sleep in the cabin instead of the tent?" she asked hopefully.

"You can suit yourself, but it's pretty old. I don't think you will want to."

Jennifer's heart sank but she still entertained the hope of spending the night in the cabin instead of the tent. They left Dark Creek and the sun had gone behind the mountains. Only a red sky remained when they spotted the little cabin in the trees and heard the rushing waters of Hospital Creek nearby. It was a great relief to Jennifer to climb down out of the saddle and inspect the cabin while Brian and Chris unloaded the pack horse after unsaddling and watering the riding horses. She pushed open the door of the cabin, and the stench of dust and mold rushed out to her. She took a cautious step inside the dark rustic interior and saw that it was very primitive. There was a little old stove that looked more like a heater than a cook stove in the centre of the room, but obviously served as both, as it had a flat top that would accommodate a couple of pots. There wasn't much else to see. A rickety table and a couple of chairs. In a dark corner two bunks were roughly attached to the wall. A hunter's cabin, or maybe a prospector, or a trapper, and she shuddered at the thought of trapping animals. What made man leave civilization and come to remote places like this? She understood that in the country's pioneer era there had been explorers with curiosity, hunters seeking food and clothing, and prospectors looking for fortunes in gold. But there must always have been some just plain mountain men like Brian. This time it was to track the ram, "for Chris," he said, but she had suspected it was for Brian too. He had been here before, many times, or he wouldn't be here now. He loved to "ride in the hills," as he called these rugged peaks, that were among some of the highest in the world. Was it to "get away from it all," or a basic need to return to nature? A need to smell the crisp fresh air on the lofty peaks, and the damp earth under the moss in the deep ravines. To hear the rushing water and trees in the swaying wind. A feast for the soul of man.

Chris was unrolling the sleeping bags, so she gave him a hand. Then she started unpacking food and cooking utensils while Chris helped Brian gather wood for a camp fire, which Brian said they could build at that time of year, as the fire season was over. They put the saddles and equipment they wouldn't be needing until morning in the little cabin. Jennifer had decided to sleep in the tent, after all. Brian wanted something to heat water in, and she couldn't understand why until he handed her a steaming mug of hot rum, which he said was a must after a strenuous day in the saddle. Chris wanted to join in when they started toasting the success of the journey so far; so Brian gave him a mug with a few drops of rum and a lot of hot water and honey, and he was happy. The delicious rum not only helped soothe their aching limbs, it assuaged their nerves which had become frayed from the clashes and grievances of the long, arduous day.

7   Fireside Chats

They ate by the light of a roaring fire after consuming a goodly quantity of Brian's rum. They wolfed down plates of delicious food, beef steak and baked potatoes done to perfection over a bed of coals from the campfire, with all the trimmings like butter and sour cream. Brian remarked that thanks to portable picnic coolers and ice, the monotony of eating only bacon and beans on the trail is long gone. Then they lay back in quiet solitude to relax after the rigors of the adventuresome day. Silver made his presence known by lounging at Christopher's feet and making little grumbling noises in his throat. Chris had already given him what few scraps were left from their own meal. It wasn't enough for the hungry dog after its strenuous day, so Chris gave him dog food as well. Brian piled more wood on the fire and they were quiet for a time, until Chris became restless and wanted to talk about Sam.

"Where do you think Sam is now, Dad?"

"He's probably spending the night safely on a rock bluff someplace."

"Dad, remember when Sam chased you up on the shed roof?" and he started to laugh.

"When we were looking after Thompson's nanny goat?" and Brian laughed a bit too, but continued in a sober tone, "the bears got the goat last summer.

Jennifer sat up and looked curious, so Brian related the story for her. "The goat was in heat and I had her tethered out in the yard. When I went to put her in the shed for the night, I picked up her leash and Sam left the corral as I started leading the goat to the shed. I was near the corral when I happened to look over my shoulder; and there was Sam with his head down ready to charge, so I jumped on the rails of the corral and up onto the shed roof. I still had the goat's leash in my hand, so I gave it a tug towards me and the goat jumped into the shed as Sam charged and hit the rails on the corral. Sam backed up and I leaned over and closed the shed door."

"You mean he liked the goat?" Jennifer asked, laughing.

"It was love at first sight. He likes the horses too; they are his herd. Farley the game warden said we would have trouble if we ever got a stallion."

"Really? He's funny, but he and Silver get along fine."

"They tolerate each other."

"Why does the game warden think he left the herd and came to the ranch?"

"They think he had a fight with another ram and lost, but I can't understand why they would be fighting in May. He came on the first of May, the day Chris was born. I had been at the hospital and when I drove through the gate I saw him coming out of the bush on the mountain side of the field. He was moving slowly and limping.

"When I stopped the truck he had disappeared behind the barn, so I went around to look, and there he was with a big gash across his chest with the blood dripping to the ground. We just stood there looking at each other. He looked like he was in pretty bad shape and I didn't think he was going to make it, but I went into the barn to get him a pail of water and some oats, and when I came back he was just lying there against the barn in the sun. I put the water and oats beside him and next morning he had eaten the oats, so I gave him some more. Eventually, he got better and stayed on, making the ranch his home except for these periods when he goes away. He hasn't always left in the fall, it's just been the last couple of years that he leaves in the fall like this. Before that he left in the summer. The game department followed him for thirty miles in a helicopter once, but he just went to some lakes in Yoho National Park."

Jennifer remembered an incident she had been curious about, so she said, "I thought he did funny things but I didn't want to say anything because I didn't think you'd believe me, but one day I was out by the barn and he was lying by the horses sleeping, and I thought the horses were watching him. Then they all moved off down towards the meadow. Just as I was going to the house, the ram came charging across the yard and over the fence after the horses. Do you think that's what happened?"

"Oh sure, he woke up and found them gone and got mad. He thinks they belong to him," Brian said.

"What a chauvinist he is," Jennifer said, laughing.

"The horses hate him." Brian was laughing too.

"Dad, tell Jennifer about the time he went through the sliding glass doors." Chris seemed to have got over his annoyance with Jennifer or else had shelved it for the night. He was enjoying the story-telling session.

"One day he saw his reflection in the sliding glass doors to the patio; at least that's what I think happened. Anyway, he charged and ended up with his head through the door. I think he realized he didn't want to go into the house because he backed up right away and took off. I think he must have felt pretty silly as we didn't see him again for a few days. He has cost me a lot of money over the years he has been at the ranch. I had to replace the door, and he uses a lot of hay, too. It's not what he eats that I mind, but he is always pulling hay into the corral for the horses, and a lot goes to waste."

"He seems to be really fond of the horses then?" Jennifer asked.

"His protective instinct towards them is incredibly strong. I was down in the meadow shooting gophers once when Bell was limping; I thought she had stepped in a gopher hole. Sam was down there with the horses and I expected him to leave at the sound of the gun, but he didn't. He was terrified; he even urinated on himself in fear but he would not leave the horses."

"Isn't that incredible? Aw, poor thing, aren't the instincts of nature strong."

Jennifer had a new compassion for Sam, even if he was the cause of her being on this miserable trip. She had forgotten about the trials of the day and was enjoying relaxing around the fire, thanks to the effects of the hot rum. Brian had expected a tirade from Jennifer at the mention of the gun, but she had overlooked it because of her concern for the sheep. He had just about given up any hope of her learning the ways of their life during the day, but it didn't seem so bad now that they were relaxing after their meal and drinks. The fire had burned down and Brian got up to put on more wood. Jennifer saw Chris stifle a yawn and realized that he was having a hard time staying awake; so she said, "Time for bed, Chris."

"No, I want to stay up longer."

"It's getting late, and we have to get up early." She saw that Brian was just watching the fire and Chris hadn't moved, so she spoke again, "I don't want any crabby boys on my hands tomorrow." Then recalling her clashes with Chris during the day she wished she hadn't said that, but it was always up to her to make Chris do as he was told, Brian let him do just as he pleased; no wonder he had changed his mind about accepting her, she thought.

When she first came to the ranch to live, she thought Brian was soft with him because he had lost his mother and it was his way of trying to make it up to him. Now she wasn't so sure. Maybe it was the way he was, or the way he and Joanne had both been. That would explain why Chris was so spoiled when she first came. Chris had seemed to accept her discipline. He even respected her for it, and turned to her for reassurance, so she thought she was doing the right thing by giving him guidelines. Now, with his newfound resentment of her, she didn't feel as if she could handle him, and if that was the case, if he was resenting her for disciplining him, then things were going to be very difficult indeed. Brian noticed that Chris wasn't making any move to do as Jennifer had told him. It was becoming one of his worries of late that he just wouldn't listen to her. He wondered if it had something to do with the boy's seemingly growing resentment toward her, or if the novelty of having her with them had worn off. He decided to give it more thought later and spoke to his son. "Do as Mom says." Even though Chris was now calling her Jennifer, Brian still referred to her as Mom.

Chris got up reluctantly and went to the tent. He lifted up the flap and said not too heartily, "Goodnight."

"No goodnight kiss?" Jennifer immediately wished she had not spoken for it was obvious that Chris wasn't going to give either of them a kiss. He had stopped doing it about the same time as he had started calling her Jennifer. She didn't know much about raising little boys and decided she would have to find out how old they were when they didn't want to be kissed any more, but when he spoke she knew he was not that old yet.

"I'm too big," he said in a voice that indicated that he was not very big at all, regardless of his size, and disappeared into the tent.

Brian and Jennifer sat quietly looking into the fire for a time, then Brian picked up a stick and started absently poking the wood in the fire, pushing it into the flame, making the fire burn brighter and the sparks to fly. When he spoke she knew he was worried about Chris again. "I thought he was better with you tonight, didn't you?" He sounded like he was hoping against hope, Jennifer thought, and for a minute she thought of going along with his hope but then decided to be honest.

"Only when he got distracted, I think. He calls me Jennifer all the time now; he never makes a mistake about that." She moved over and rested her head on Brian's arm. He was lost to her when he started thinking about the problem with Chris, and she resented it. "Don't worry so much about it; it will work out, I'm sure." She wished she felt as confident as she sounded.

Brian put his arm around her and drew her close to him. She wanted so much to tell him her news and nearly did, but realized that this wasn't the time. They sat cuddled together for a while gazing into the fire, lost in thought. A breeze came up and stirred the fire, sending sparks into the dark sky. When they fell on the grass, the dew extinguished them. When Brian removed his arm and said it was time to turn in, Jennifer was disappointed. There was nothing romantic about sleeping bags, especially with Chris sharing the tent with them, and she grimaced in annoyance as she went to the tent while Brian banked the fire for the night.

Christopher was sound asleep when Brian and Jennifer crawled into their sleeping bags beside him in the little tent, and it wasn't long until Brian's breathing indicated that he had no trouble falling asleep. Jennifer was very tired and she ached all over, but she couldn't go to sleep. She was thinking of how much more complicated life had become since she met Brian.

When they first met, Gail was thrilled that they were "hitting it off," as she put it. She was all excited about her matchmaking until they announced that they were getting married, then she changed. Jennifer couldn't understand it, as that was exactly what Gail had said she wanted.

She could hear her asking as she always did, in one of their long visits on the phone, the year after her sister died, "Any serious relationship yet? No, good. I'm saving you for Brian when he's ready." She called her a lot that year. Jennifer thought it was because she was in a state of mourning and needed someone to talk to. She laughed at Gail's concern for Brian and Christopher's loneliness and didn't take any of it seriously. Jennifer was deeply involved with her music at UBC and the opera at the time, and had no intention of spoiling it all by getting married. But it was summer and in the evenings and on weekends she was lonely and restless. Brian was only taking one course at the university and had lots of time to spend with her. They swam in the ocean and tanned on the beach in the sun. They took Chris to the children's zoo in Stanley Park, and to Exhibition Park where he was thrilled with the rides and wanted to try every one.

They went for outings to Horseshoe Bay, and up the Sunshine Coast, and dined everywhere from McDonalds, which Chris loved, to the most exotic places they could find. They played tennis and found they were an even match; Brian had a bit of an edge, so that was fine. He won a few more times than Jennifer did. And by the end of the summer Jennifer was deeply in love with Brian Logan. But it wasn't until he went home to

Golden that she knew she couldn't live without him. He was her man. She loved his strength and courage, his generosity, and most of all the way he could make her laugh when she wanted to cry. In October she went to Golden to meet his family. She visited Windsong where they were to live. She was so in love with Brian that she saw everything with a rosy glow. She thought his family were the most wonderful people she had ever met, and Windsong the most beautiful place she had ever seen.

At Christmas Brian came to Vancouver and gave her a beautiful solitaire that he had chosen himself and she loved it. He explained to her that their way of life was hard and she might find it difficult, but she was so determined to share his life that she convinced him that she would love it too. They were married in June and she had come to the ranch to live. At first she was a happy bride, thrilled with each new adventure.

She was sure that it was when Christopher had started school that his resentment towards her had occured. Tired and lying awake in the little tent while the others slept, she almost hated Chris at that moment. The burning sensation that comes from withheld tears scorched her throat. The wind grew stronger. She could hear it singing in the tree tops, and it seemed to be saying to her "be patient." It was lulling her to sleep, like Windsong. She thought, I've come to love the sound of the wind singing at Windsong; they named it well. And she fell into a deep sleep with a determination to succeed.

8   Thoughts from the Past

Brian was up early. He emerged from the tent in time to see a white tail deer and two fawns bound from the creek where they had been drinking. He stretched and yawned and then shivered in the cold. There was no sign of the coming sun and the ground was covered with such a heavy dew he thought at first it was frost. He reached back into the tent for his jacket and then went to check on the horses, who looked refreshed after their night's rest. Silver wandered out from the little cabin where he spent the night and followed Brian down to the creek when he went to water the horses.

As Brian stood holding the halters while the horses drank slowly from the icy waters of the creek, he dreamily recalled his first wife, Joanne. He marvelled at the way nature had of healing. The trauma of Joanne's illness in the years following Christopher's birth was fading and he was remembering only the happy times. And he was deluding himself into thinking she had died when Chris was born, leaving him with their baby to raise, but in reality that was not how it had happened.

He was having his morning coffee in the kitchen at Windsong when Joanne walked in all smiles. "I'm having contractions, honey, so maybe you better take me to the hospital on your way to school." Brian was about to jump up and rush her to the hospital when he remembered the instructions from the prenatal classes and calmed down. When she was settled at the hospital, she looked calm and happy. She kissed him and said, "You may as well go on to school. I'm fine. Babies take a long time to come, especially the first one; the nurse can call you when things start to happen."

"Are you sure, dear? You know I want to be with you at the time." Brian was reluctant to leave her, but it was a bit late to get a substitute, so with misgivings, he left her.

He phoned the hospital at noon and was told his wife was coming along fine. After school he went to the hospital, and Joanne was still being brave and told him she was fine and that things were progressing normally. But he could see that she was getting uncomfortable, so he made up his mind not to leave her until it was all over. They brought him some supper when they brought Joanne's tray, but she was too uncomfortable to eat anything, and they both kept saying it shouldn't be much longer. Brian slept for a few hours on the couch in the waiting room when they gave Joanne something to make her sleep, but she was in worse pain when she woke up.

The doctor examined her again in the morning, but made no comment. She was trying very hard to follow the breathing exercises they had learned at prenatal classes, and Brian was trying to assist her, but nothing helped. She was sure that this was the way it was supposed to be, and Brian was becoming more and more sure as time went on that it was not the way it was supposed to be.

Joanne gave him a wan smile and said, "You may as well go to school, and they can call you."

"I'm not leaving you, so don't even mention it," Brian said and went and called the school to get a sub for him for the day. Then he sat and held Joanne's hand and talked about everything he could think of to keep her mind off her pain. By afternoon she was suffering terribly he could see, although she was trying to hide it. He became frightened.

When the doctor examined her again, he informed Brian that he would have to do a caesarean section, and Brian felt both relief and fear. Fear of the unknown and relief that the ordeal would soon be over. He paced the floor while she was in the operating room, and then nearly went out of his mind when he saw his parents and sister arrive.

"She hemorrhaged when they removed the placenta," Russell Logan's voice was stiff with emotion, "and they are not sure if they can save her." His sister Cheryl put her arms around Brian and kissed his cheek before she spoke in a trembling voice, "The baby is fine, it's a boy, and he weighed ten and a half pounds. He was too big for her to deliver." Brian was on the verge of despair at the thought that he might lose Joanne, but they saved her, and he was lifted from despair. And then he lost her anyway. He lost her through a terrible illness—that was the irony of it.

It must have been talking about the ram the night before that caused him to recall the whole thing in its entirety. It had flashed before him when he was telling Jennifer about coming home and finding the ram at Windsong, with his chest all torn open, and the blood running and soaking into the ground right after Joanne had lost so much blood. He had felt at the time it was an omen that there was more suffering to come, and he had been right. He had lost Joanne, and it hadn't ended there; he still missed her.

They had been well matched. Both teachers, they loved Windsong and to ride in the hills. Too perfect. He should have known it couldn't last. Someone had said; "People as sweet and wonderful as Joanne are not meant for this world." The description fit her perfectly. Brian remembered at one time or another that every member of her family had expressed their concern for her being so vulnerable to people. She never did anything to hurt anyone. No wonder she was adored. Everyone in Golden had loved her, and said she gave them the feeling that she couldn't protect herself, and yet she had been strong and determined to achieve her goals.

Brian looked across the creek at the bushes where the doe and fawns had disappeared, and thought of how Joanne would have loved it here, and pictured her face, smiling. How beautiful she had been with her long blonde hair and big blue eyes. Her sister, Lynn, said she knew their baby would have blue eyes and blond hair before he was born. How could he miss when his parents had the same coloring. It had all been too perfect. Life wasn't meant to be that way. Their families still had nothing but respect for each other.

His parents and sister loved Joanne, and he still loved her family like his own. Her mother, Madeline, was wise and kind, and Roger, her father, who was generous to a fault, had asked him to call them by their first names. In spite of their loyalty to Joanne, her parents, her sister Lynn, and her brother Don all approved of his marriage to Jennifer. On the other hand, Gail's friendship with Jennifer had cooled after she brought them together. And he never understood why.

The horses finished drinking and stepped back from the creek, bringing Brian's thoughts back to the present situation at hand. They had to have a bit to eat, break up camp, and be on their way again. As he came up the bank from the creek with the horses Chris, who was up and dressed, was doing a pretty good job of trying to start the camp fire; so Brian let him do it, while he got the coffee ready.

Jennifer smelled the coffee. It was the one thing that got her up in the morning. In fact, it was the only thing that got her up in the morning. Jennifer loved to sleep, and she seemed to enjoy it the most when it was time to get up.

"Come and get it," Chris called while he banged on the bottom of a pan with a stick outside the tent.

"Giving her the traditional call to breakfast by the camp-fire, are you?" Brian asked.

Then in a more impatient voice Chris said, "We gotta hurry up so we can catch up to Sam. Come on, Jennifer."

"OK, don't be in such a hurry; I'm coming," Jennifer said as she dressed in warm clothes and joined them for a quick bite and cup of coffee. She was pleased to see Brian had filled the thermos to take along.

Brian had the horses saddled and ready, and Chris took down the little tent and rolled up the sleeping bags, while Jennifer packed up the breakfast things. Brian loaded Nelliebell and they were ready to go. In the cold morning air, they mounted up and rode off in search of the trail left by the ram. Silver knew Sam's spore by now, so after some circling around and sniffing along the route they had left the night before to find the little cabin, he started barking and running along Hospital Creek. The riders followed.

Unknown to the worried family, the ram spent the night in a little thicket on a rocky bluff just above their camp.

As they came out of the trees into a clearing the sun was rising and Brian remarked that it looked like they would have another beautiful Indian summer day, and Chris wanted to know what Indian summer was.

"I don't know, do you, Brian? Other than it's a warm spell like summer in the fall before winter comes," and at the thought of winter, her dread of it returned.

"I think the Indians called it the God of the Southwest, Cautantowwit. One story says that the settlers named it after the Indians, who looked forward to the period and told the settlers about it, and another story says the Indians used the period to make more attacks on the settlers, which is suggested by the tradition of the carved pumpkin at Halloween being put in the window to scare the Indians away.

"Anyway, it's a pretty nice time of year in the hills. There isn't the dampness that there is in the spring, and when it gets dry in the summer, there is the forest closure and you can't go anyway." Brian was starting to enjoy himself again. He stopped his horse and took the binoculars from their case to scan the mountainside ahead, but there was no sign of Sam. This worried Brian. He hoped that Silver hadn't made a mistake, but didn't believe that a dog could once it knew a scent. It was possible that it wasn't Sam whom Silver was following. Maybe he was following a coyote. But then there were lots of worse things he could be following such as, let's see, he thought, wolves or a bear or a cougar, but he didn't think the dog would follow a cougar. It might just be a deer or an elk or a caribou.

He looked at Jennifer as she rode up beside him and was glad she couldn't read his thoughts. He looked at Chris too, to see if he realized that they had not caught sight of Sam at least once since leaving home yesterday morning. There had been tracks, but there was no proof that they were Sam's, except for the ones near the creek above the ranch. He was sure no other sheep would come that close to civilization. He swallowed to relieve the dryness in his throat. He nudged Glory to move on while he contemplated what he would do if they didn't catch up to the ram. Chris would be heartbroken, maybe even more. There was something else behind his intense desire to go where Sam goes, and Brian wanted to find out what that something was, and in order to do that he had to find that darn ram. If he had looked a minute sooner, he would have seen the ram enter a clump of trees not too far ahead of them.

Instead he was wishing that he had talked Jennifer into staying at home, because without her along, he and Chris could have made twice as good time. He had hoped she would learn to love riding and the outdoors like he and Chris did, but from yesterday's happenings she hadn't learned to enjoy any of it, he was disappointed.

As Brian rode he looked around. He looked at the cliffs ahead with their jutting rocks, at the colored leaves, and felt the warmth of the autumn sun, and thought, it's all gold in the fall; everything shines like gold, and it makes me melancholy. It possessed him. He let it seep into him and replenish his soul.

Each summer the suffering came, as that is when he had lost her, and he let it overpower him. When the fall came the winter would follow. He could draw inside and light the fire to keep out the cold, and the memories. He could lie in bed at night and listen to the wind whistle around the corners of the house and under the eaves, while it swept the snow into drifts across the yard and down the road. And then he and Chris would have to get out to North Bench Road by snowmobile to go to school, until he could get the cat out and plow the road through the trees from the ranch to North Bench. The road was on his own property, and he had to maintain it himself. He loved working with the cat. It gave him a good feeling, pushing snow around, like building castles in the sand when you're a kid, he thought. Clearing snow was good therapy.

Brian had started looking forward to the winters the last couple of years. They seemed to have a numbing effect on the pain, the old regrets. He could put it away for another year. When would it be gone? Time heals, they say. Is time healing?

he wondered. Was the pain less each year? Sometimes the pain was so intense he thought it would never leave. And then there was Chris. Chris the reminder. Chris who was so much a part of him, and whom he found so hard to understand sometimes.

Christopher Cyrus they named him. Joanne wanted to call him Christopher, and he wanted to call him Cyrus. Christopher first, she said, the protector of travelers. Was it fate, or did she have a premonition? She did say life was a journey. And because of Christopher they were making a journey into the hills to follow Sam. Brian felt that he had taken some wrong turns, but he had come back and started again, searching, searching everywhere, for what? What are we all searching for? Happiness, fulfilment, that's it. Do we ever find it? Yes, he had found it but it hadn't lasted, damn it. Fate had seen to that, and at that moment the poignancy of his loss was more than he could bear. And he seemed to hear his cousin's voice singing on their wedding day, "Walk hand in hand with me, through all eternity." They had been married on Boxing Day, the day after Christmas, as Joanne was finishing her teacher's training at UBC that year and they wanted to go to Lake Louise to ski on their honeymoon. It had been a candlelight ceremony with all her attendants wearing long red velvet dresses, which made Joanne's beauty stand out even more in her trailing white gown. She had been radiant, and his cousin Greg sang, his powerful voice rising to the rafters of the church. But what did it mean, through all eternity? He thought it meant it would be forever, eternity was forever. Although it hadn't been forever, in the meantime, his feelings were with her.

"Dad," Chris called, "You're gettin' way ahead of us. Jennifer can't keep up!"

Brian was jarred out of his reverie. He turned to see Chris and Jennifer just emerging from the last stand of trees they had passed through.

"Jennifer," he called in annoyance, "get that damn horse moving. You are letting her go to sleep." He felt pangs of guilt. How were he and Jennifer going to make it when his emotions were so divided?

Jennifer nudged Bess in the flank with her heel and she

stepped more lively. "It's you, Brian," she called. "You're just going too fast, like we're not even here." Brian knew that Chris could keep up to almost any pace he set, but had stayed behind due to his concern for Jennifer's welfare. He was afraid she might get lost and they would have to spend their time looking for her instead of following Sam. He had mentioned it to Brian when they were alone in the early morning before Jennifer got up. At that moment Brian wondered what he was doing married to a singer, and an opera singer at that. He could hear his grandfather Logan when he had come home from UBC to tell him that he was getting married to Joanne, "Don't marry a city girl, Brian. She will never love Windsong like we do."

"But she's not a city girl, Grandpa," Brian had said, "She was raised in the West Kootenays, in Creston, before her parents sold their business and moved to Vancouver." And Grandpa Logan had loved Joanne with all his heart.

Brian wondered what he would say if he knew he was married to a city girl now, one who sang in the opera. Turn over in his grave, no doubt. Then Brian felt more guilty than ever, for Jennifer had been good to them. She had put a great deal of effort into being a wife and mother, and he had admired her for it. It wasn't easy for her, he knew, to suddenly have a husband and son to look after, after being single for thirty years.

He had been pleased when Chris started calling her Mom. It had pleased her too, and it looked like they were getting to be a real family until about the time Chris started school, and it had Brian worried. It wasn't that Chris disliked Jennifer, he didn't think. It was more that he wasn't going to accept her as a mother, and seemed to resent her being at Windsong. He didn't want her coming on the trip, Brian knew that. And if Chris wouldn't tell him what was wrong, and Chris wouldn't, not yet anyway, then he was just going to have to be patient with him and maybe things would work out. There was nothing like a good trip up into the mountains to assuage people's emotions.

They were following Hospital Creek up a draw between the two mountains, and at this altitude some of the trees were already bare skeletons against the rich blue of the autumn sky.

Their leaves lay thick and colorful on the ground, but fluttered around when they were disturbed by the feet of the passing horses. A sound much louder than the rustle of the leaves reached their ears, and Jennifer wondered what it was.

"Brian, what is that roar? Don't tell me we are still close enough to the railroad to hear the train. I can't believe it."

"No, that is Hospital Falls up ahead, and they are a pretty sight. You will enjoy seeing them." And if she didn't, he thought, he would have to give up all hope that she would learn to enjoy living at Windsong and riding in the hills with them.

The sound became a deafening roar, and as they rode out of the trees, the falls came into view. It was a beautiful sight. They stopped the horses and dismounted to watch the water cascading down over the rocks to the pool below, where the crimson leaves drifted while the cedars that were reflected in the water displayed their majestic green.

"Oh, how beautiful it is!" Jennifer's voice was just a whisper above the sound of the falling water. "I love it." Brian was surprised and pleased that she was enjoying the sight. It was the first time she had shown any appreciation of the magnificent scenery they had seen along the way, and Brian's heart warmed towards her.

"I thought you would enjoy this," he said as he put his arm around her shoulders. She loved his arm around her. The sound of the water roaring over the falls and the sight of the scarlet leaves on the pond with the reflection of green from the trees underneath was filling Jennifer with a feeling of tranquility when Chris broke the spell.

"Dad, when do you think we are going to see Sam? We keep stopping all the time so Jennifer can look at things." Brian dropped his arm from around Jennifer's shoulders. "There's a place up ahead where we can scan the whole side of both mountains; we should be able to spot him then." Brian hoped they could, because if they didn't he was going to start to get very uneasy about finding the sheep.

The inference in Christopher's voice that it was all her fault that they hadn't caught up to Sam had its effect on Jennifer. She felt like she didn't belong again. It annoyed her that she could feel that way about her husband and a boy she had started to love like a son. And then she remembered how annoyed she felt when Gail made a fuss when she and Brian announced that they were getting married.

She had started to panic, in fear of losing Brian before she really had him, but wanted desperately to have him. She became more determined when Gail started acting like he belonged to her. Jennifer felt in order for him to belong to her she must first take him away from the people he was associating with when he was at the coast. The old friends that he and Joanne had gone to university with, where they met, and her family. Joanne's family especially, seemed like a threat to her chance of gaining Brian's love. At first she couldn't understand the deep ties Brian had with the Forbes, and thought it was not just that they were Christopher's grandparents but because of Joanne, and she resented this. Later, she learned that he sometimes called Madeline Forbes "Mom" and that he loved her. She suspected that it was due to losing his own mother when he was in his teens, and his father having remarried.

Brian was not very close to his stepmother. But whatever the reason for his attachment to the Forbes, Jennifer had learned that in order to have Brian at all she had to accept them. Jennifer had liked the Forbes when she and Gail were friends at college. But after the words she had with Gail over Brian, the Forbes became a threat to her relationship with him. Later she learned that they did not compare her to Joanne as she had feared, but accepted her for herself and that there was a place for her in their hearts.

That was not the way with Brian's family. Brian was very close to his father and sister Cheryl, but Jennifer found his father reserved and hard to reach. His sister made her feel that she would never take the place of Joanne, which Jennifer had no intention of doing. She wanted desperately to find a place of her own, and found it ironic that Brian's stepmother, who was in a similar position to her, was no help at all. She was such a quiet, passive person that Jennifer had difficulty communicating with her, so that their relationship had become one of polite acceptance. She wondered if the attitude of his grandparents and aunt towards her had anything to do with Christopher's growing resentment of her, and thought wearily of mentioning the possibility of it to Brian. She was so engrossed in her thoughts that she hadn't noticed Brian and Chris mount up until Chris said, "What are we waiting for? We are never going to catch up to Sam, we are going too slow."

"Come on, let's go," Brian said irritably, letting Jennifer know that the pleasant moment they had spent when he put his arm around her had passed.

Jennifer climbed on Bess so fast she nearly fell off the other side. Both Brian and Chris wore looks of impatience at her inept horsemanship, and apparent inability to learn. This aroused a fierce determination within her to show them. It was too late for her to turn around and go home by herself. She couldn't possibly find her way, and there was no hope of getting Brian and Chris to turn back. She felt that they were on a wild goose chase. They would never find that damn sheep which was the cause of all her misery; so she may as well make the best of it and master the knack of riding a horse, just to show that smug pair ahead of her that she could do it. She was never going riding in Brian's hills again ever, and therefore would have no further need of horsemanship, baah. Horse-womanship, hurrah.

Jennifer watched Brian riding ahead. She clung to his every move. It fascinated her the way he seemed to be one with the horse and glued to the saddle. He seemed remote to her after the rebuking tone he had used when she hadn't mounted up. Then Christopher moved into view and blocked Brian out. I'll never have him, she thought, Chris is between us, or was there something else? Jennifer knew that she had taken it for granted that after she and Brian were married the three of them would become a family unit. She had pictured dinners with the three of them around the table, Christmas with the three of them around the tree, but it wasn't turning out that way, and she was hurt and disappointed. How often did he recall his life with Joanne, she wondered. Even before the trouble with Chris, she saw him engrossed in thought and feared he had not recovered from his loss, but believed he would in time. She knew she must not resent Chris or she would lose Brian forever.

They were a unit, a strong family unit, and she was still an outsider. Then, she decided, Brian is trying to be both parents to Chris instead of letting her be one, except for disciplining Chris. Brian let her do that, or did he? Maybe he didn't like the way she handled Chris. He was trying to get closer to his son to try to understand him. That's why he was taking him on this trip, to try to communicate with him better.

All three needed to learn how to communicate better, she thought. She wondered what it took to become a family with a child who was not her own. Just getting married didn't do it. It was not that simple, she knew that now. Gail had been right. Maybe she was her friend, after all, and had been trying to tell her something that would have saved her a lot of heartache. But Jennifer hadn't listened.

9   On the Right Track

They came out of the woods onto a bluff that gave them a sweeping view of the side of two mountains. "Where are we, Brian? I am completely lost," Jennifer asked with determination, trying to show him her interest in the search.

"Get that thermos of coffee and I will draw you a map while we have a cup."

"No," Chris said, "I want to keep going. We'll never catch up to Sam if we keep stopping all the time."

"Here," Brian said as he took the binoculars off the saddle and handed them to Chris. "You can look around for him while we have a break. We have been riding for hours, and the horses need a rest."

They let the horses stand while they sat on a log drinking their coffee and Chris scanned the mountainside in search of Sam. "Is that Hospital Creek down there below us?" Jennifer asked in a bold voice.

"No, that's Glenogle Creek," Brian answered civilly, respecting her attitude. "I'll show you." He picked up a stick, scraped his boot along the ground to clear a bare spot to the earth and started to sketch. "Here is Windsong." He made a mark in the dirt with the stick. "We followed the little creek on the ranch, Meadow Creek, I call it, as it feeds the pond in the meadow. Okay, we followed it up along the side of the mountain behind the ranch, where you saw the old cabins. Then we went down and followed the Kicking Horse River to Dark Creek that runs into the Kicking Horse, here, and we followed that old logging road to Hospital Creek and stayed at the cabin, about here," and he drew in the dirt with the stick. "Then we followed Hospital Creek to its source pretty well. Now we have crossed over to Glenogle, then there is Porcupine Creek, and if we keep going in this direction we will soon be in the Park and there will be the Otterhead River to cross, and the next thing you know we might end up at Emerald Lake." He had stopped drawing in the dirt with the stick and was pointing in the direction of the creek and the mountains beyond with a lust for adventure in his voice and gleam in his eye.

"I would love to see Emerald Lake, but it sounds like a long way," she said, but didn't add—by driving there in a car, sometime.

"If Sam goes, we're going," Chris said, and turned to give Jennifer a "that's enough out of you" look, and then as defiance grew in his eyes it was as if he added, "shut up, too" and he went back to scanning the mountain for Sam.

Jennifer got his message, but didn't care. The mention of crossing a river had unnerved her, and she thought someone should pay heed to the distance they were getting away from home and the time it was taking. "But we have been a day and a half already; how can we do it over the weekend if we keep going like this?" When she saw the look of determination that came over Brian's face, she knew she may as well have spoken to the wind. In fact, it would have been better for her if she had, for he was annoyed at her again. It was in his voice when he spoke.

"We are going to do it, however long it takes. What's an extra day?" And Chris turned around again and gave her a withering look, but didn't feel he had to say anything further after the tone of voice he had heard his father use.

At that moment Brian was more lost to her than ever. This was a Brian she hadn't known before they were married, a mountain man, she thought, a breed she wasn't sure she could cope with. Brian got up and went to stand by Chris.

"Any sign of Sam yet?"

"No, I can't find him." What they didn't know was that this wise, wild sheep, even though he spent most of the year at the ranch, was now in his natural environment and was using his instincts and his keen sight and hearing to hide from them, and again they had just missed seeing him enter a thicket.

Silver started barking off in the trees, so both males went to see what the ruckus was about and called to Jennifer to join them. Silver had a squirrel up a tree, and the squirrel was sitting on a limb, looking down at the dog with his beady little eyes and a saucy tilt to his head. Silver was very annoyed and had his front paws on the trunk of the tree as if to climb up after his prey, but the squirrel continued eating the nut it had carried up in its little claws and dropping the chaff on Silver's head.

"That is about the biggest squirrel I've ever seen, just look at the size of his tail," Brian remarked. Even the size of a squirrel has become important, Jennifer thought. What affects men when they get out in the wilds, she wondered. Then she had to admit it was curious watching the cheeky little squirrel defy the dog, who was ten times its size, once it had reached the safety of the tree where the dog couldn't follow.

They walked back to the clearing. Jennifer emptied the thermos into their mugs. Brian went over to the edge of the bluff and studied the side of the mountain across the creek. He just looked and didn't say anything, but he was praying that he would catch sight of the sheep.

"Can you see Sam?" Chris asked, his voice anxious. When Brian didn't answer, Chris started pulling on his sleeve. "Can't you see him yet, Dad? You said we would see him when we got here."

"I thought we would, but he must be hiding in some trees or something, but Silver knows where he is going. He has picked up his trail again. Let's follow along."

The dog seemed to know where he was going and Brian hoped it was after Sam. When he sat down and drew the route they had taken for Jennifer, it had become obvious that whatever Silver was tracking was taking the shortest way to the park by following the creeks for food and water. But he thought he had best keep his thoughts to himself; no use alarming Jennifer that they might go all the way to the park.

After they followed the dog along the bluff for a time they came to a gentle slope that went down to the creek.

"We may as well get off and walk for a while and save the horses," Brian suggested.

"Good idea." Jennifer was all for walking. She was sore from the riding they had done the day before, and the stretch they had put in the saddle that morning hadn't done anything to relieve her aching body.

"No. I don't want to walk, it's too slow. We'll never catch up to Sam this way." Chris sounded almost tearful, and Jennifer saw the muscle along Brian's jaw tighten.

"It will do us good to walk for a while and the horses too," Brian said as he got off and started leading his horse down the gentle slope.

It was fairly clear of shrub so Jennifer walked beside Brian leading Bess, and Chris, after sitting on Jingle for a time with a thunderous look on his face, followed reluctantly. Jennifer could feel the atmosphere growing tense and decided that what they needed was some conversation to take their minds off Sam.

"Brian, how about telling us about that relative of yours who was involved in the bootlegging business. It looks like we can walk side by side for a while, and I like old stories." Besides, she had irritated Brian enough on the trip, and with her lack of knowledge of riding and the wilds she was likely to do so further. She thought if he told them another one of his stories that he loved telling it would ease the tension that was building between the three of them, and make him think better of her, as well.

Brian laughed a sharp, unsteady laugh. "You want me to tell you about the black sheep in the Logan closet so you can hold it over my head, I suppose. No chance," he said jokingly.

"I won't hold it over your head. I don't know anything about my relatives. There could be some pretty bad ones for all I know. My mother tells me that my relatives in England are descendants of kings, and my father says he is descended from nothing but the best in Czechoslovakia, like university professors and statesmen." She laughed.

"Oh really. How come you didn't tell me all this before?" Brian said teasingly.

"Because it's not true, I'm just joking. I don't think either of them know much about their backgrounds at all. That's why I'm so interested in yours."

"Well, let's see, where shall I begin? Uncle Royd, or more rightly, Great Uncle Royd?"

"Forget it," Jennifer said, "you have me totally confused already; some kind of uncle, okay." Chris behind them chuckled a bit, so Jennifer pleaded, "On with the story." The more they walked, the closer to home they would stay. If Brian got involved in telling them a long-winded story, they would walk as long as Chris remained quiet. Besides, her "rear end" had had enough of the saddle for a while. So Brian continued, "Golden was quite a town in the Roaring Twenties with all the logging and sawmills, trappers and mining claims around. It was a big centre for the C.P.R., too. Just before prohibition came in, when everybody came to town on Saturday night there was a sherif who patrolled the streets with a wheel barrel to assist anybody who had lost their sense of equilibrium."

Jennifer gave a hearty laugh, Brian laughed too, and Chris joined in whether he understood or not.

"Anyway, there was a great opportunity for bootleggers in those days. First they had prohibition in the States, and they bootlegged it from Canada. Then about the time they got rid of it over there, Canada voted it in, so the bootlegging boys were back in business again, only they were bringing it from the States to Canada, and you can imagine the business there must have been in a place like Golden with all the miners and lumberjacks around. Besides, money was plentiful before the crash. Anyway, this here so-called uncle of mine (Brian had adopted the language of western movies for the benefit of his listeners) got himself into the business and holed up in one of those old cabins that you saw above Windsong, much to Grandpa Logan's distress, for he was a very law-abiding citizen, and it being a relative of his and his loving wife, Effie, he didn't know what to do about it."

"Cut the antics, Brian, and just tell the story." Jennifer tried to sound serious but couldn't keep the laughter out of her voice, for she was starting to find it rather pleasant walking along beside Glenogle Creek in the fall sunshine, while the man she so dearly loved entertained her with a story of his ancestors.

"I should tell you about the paddle wheelers on the Columbia River; you would like that better."

"I want to hear about Uncle Royd. I like him," Chris chimed in.

"Royd was Grandpa's brother. He followed Cyrus out from Ontario after he settled in Golden. Okay, when Effie became almost ill from being upset about the rumors that were going around Golden about Royd, Grandpa got furious and decided to check for himself to see if the rumors were true. He rode up to the cabin one night from Windsong, and slipped up unnoticed, and caught Royd red-handed with the contraband. Grandpa exploded and threatened to expose him if he didn't leave the country. The next thing any of the family heard of Royd was a Christmas card some years later from San Francisco, where he was living in style with a wife and family. And, to my knowledge, that is the last anyone ever heard of him."

"Well, if we ever go to San Francisco, it might be fun to look them up." It would be more along her idea of adventure, Jennifer thought.

They walked down the slope to Glenogle Creek while Brian was telling the story. The creek ran down a draw between two mountains that Brian said was part of the Van Horne range, and the terrain along the creek was a gradual incline so they were able to ride again. Silver splashed across the creek to do some exploring on the other side, which caused Brian some concern as he thought the sheep had gone that way and it would be impossible for them to follow. It was too steep for them to climb and out of the question to take the horses. He recognized it as just the kind of area that sheep inhabit. Sheer rock bluffs where they are safe from other wild animals, as they can plunge down cliffs hundreds of feet high to escape from wolves and coyotes, due to the soft pads on the bottom of their feet that act like suction cups on the rocks. He hoped he would be able to explain this to Chris if need be, but Silver bounded back across the creek to join them, much to Brian's relief.

Brian was fascinated with anything to do with the gold rush days in British Columbia. Glenogle Creek narrowed and washed over the rocky juttings from the cliff on the other side. The side they were on was turning into a steep bank. It looked to him like just the place some old prospector would have been panning for gold in days gone by. He had read at length about Fort Steele in the southern part of the Kootenays. It had been established by the North West Mounted Police before the gold rush at Wild Horse Creek near there.

Brian and his cousin Greg had a claim of their own over in the Selkirk Mountains that they checked out every summer except for that year, he had missed it because of his marriage to Jennifer. He hoped that this trip into the hills would make up for it, but if they didn't catch up to the sheep soon, the trip could turn out to be a disaster. He wished again that Jennifer had not wanted to come. There was no doubt that she was holding them up, and as he turned to look at her, he could see that she was already showing signs of weariness and it was only noon.

It was a cooler day than the one before had been, and they were still wearing their jackets. Jennifer was hungry and thirsty. She wanted to stop for lunch, but since the fun they shared when Brian told them about Uncle Royd, there had been silence between the riders, and she was afraid to mention stopping in case of a rebuff from Chris as on the day before. Although she had resolved to defy both of them and their horses, she didn't want to go asking for trouble. It looked to her as if father and son could ride on forever or until their horses gave out, and when that thought entered her mind she perked up and wondered how long horses could last and decided that she, at any rate, would not last that long, so the horses would be of no help to her.

Pangs of hunger so distracted her that she dropped a rein, which her horse promptly stepped on and stopped. She leaned over to try to retrieve the rein and nearly fell out of the saddle. She was stationary while Brian and Chris were getting further and further ahead of her. Her decision to take care of herself vanished and she called to Brian to stop in a voice edged with panic. He shook his head in disbelief and after retrieving the rein said, "We may as well stop for lunch."

Chris didn't object, but was giving Jennifer the familiar looks of contempt which she hoped were due to her inability to capture the knack of riding a horse rather than his simple contempt for her as a human being.

They ate in silence that was thick with tension, for nobody, it seemed, was even going to mention that they had not seen Sam yet. And then Brian spoke.

"You and Chris stay here. I am going to ride on up ahead for a bit to see if there is any sign of Sam."

"I want to come too. Jennifer can stay here by herself," Chris said petulantly.

"No. I want you to stay, and Silver too. I might have a better chance of seeing Sam if I go alone."

"All right then, I'll stay, but come right back if you see him," Chris said with reluctance.

As Brian rode away he was a bit disappointed in Jennifer. He had looked forward all winter and spring for her to come to live with them at Windsong, and the pleasure he would have in teaching her to ride and to enjoy the way of life he loved. He remembered how thrilled Joanne had been at seeing Windsong. How he loved her dependence on him to help her at first, and how quickly she had learned to ride and to love their outdoor life.

He could not help but feel that it wasn't so much that Jennifer couldn't learn to ride as that she didn't want to. She didn't seem to take it seriously, he thought, which meant she didn't care. It was pretty careless of her dropping a rein like that. And now the seed of doubt in Brian's mind was starting to grow, and he wondered again what really had turned Chris against her, and he became more determined than ever to find the sheep for his son.

After Brian had ridden out of sight Jennifer and Chris sat on the rocks at the side of the creek in silence. She thought of speaking to him and trying to make him understand how it was for her, and that she was really trying to learn how to ride, but when she saw the sullen look on his face she knew it was useless to even try. There wasn't much to see from where they were sitting. The jutting rocks on the cliff across the creek and the sky where the autumn blue was turning grey from haze forming, dulling the rays of the sun. She turned her gaze to the more pleasant sight of water churning over the rocks in the creek. To the foam that was forming on the crest of the waves and floating on to the still ponds where they looked like soap suds, until the bubbles burst. She was being lulled by the melody of the creek when a sound made her look at the steep bank directly behind them. Some rocks were starting to slide down the bank, gathering momentum and raising so much dust she couldn't see what was happening. Jennifer was instantly in motion, propelled by instinct. She jumped up and grabbed Chris with one hand and the bridle of his horse, which was close by, with the other. Without thinking of her own safety, she started pulling with all her might on the bridle of the horse and screaming for Brian at the top of her lungs. Silver barked frantically; Bess bolted when Jennifer screamed. They all scrambled to safety as a large portion of the bank thundered down upon the rocks on which they had been sitting.

Brian raced back to them when he heard Jennifer scream, his heart pounding in fear of what awaited him beside the creek. He was greatly relieved to see Chris and Jennifer clinging to each other at the edge of the slide while the horses were stepping around in frightened alarm, and the dog circled them all. He leapt to the ground and gathered them both in his arms, and kept asking over and over if they were all right, as they kept assuring him that they were. They led the horses away from the slide and the narrow banks that enclosed the creek, and entered a clearing where the creek spread out in a little mountain meadow.

"Jennifer saved me, Dad, Jennifer saved me," Chris said over and over. Brian was ashamed of ever having doubted

Jennifer. He was stupid to have been angry with her just because she hadn't mastered the knack of riding a horse.

They were recovering from their near tragedy in the safety of the meadow and discussing it to help relieve the fright it had given them.

"How did you happen to see it coming?" Brian asked Jennifer. "I heard something. I guess it was the sound of the rocks bouncing and it drew my attention. I didn't know what was happening. I never saw anything like it in my life and it scared me," she said in a voice that still shook with fear.

"It was a lucky thing that you perceived something drastic was happening," Brian said in admiration

"Did you see Sam, Dad?" Chris asked, forgetting the incident, so keen was his anxiety over finding the sheep.

"I didn't have time to go far enough to see anything when I heard Jennifer," he said.

They were still standing in the meadow waiting for the horses to settle down when Jennifer turned around and saw an animal standing at the far end of the meadow watching them. It moved slightly and she saw it was a sheep and thought it must be Sam. She watched entranced at the object of their search, and then spoke softly, not wanting to frighten him off before the others saw him.

"Sam is at the other end of the meadow watching us."

Brian and Chris turned to look in disbelief, and saw that it really was Sam, standing watching them.

When Chris saw his beloved animal standing in the meadow he was so excited he could not contain himself. He called out, "Sam!" and started to run towards him, but the sheep turned at Christopher's approach and ran the other way, disappearing into the bushes. Chris stopped in disappointment and stood in the meadow calling, "Sam, Sam," but the sheep was gone.

After his mother died Chris was very lonely. When Brian was away at school and Hazel the nanny was there, Chris would sit under the table with a picture of his mother and cry. When Hazel took the picture away, he went out into the yard and followed Sam around talking to him about his mother. Chris felt the sheep understood his feelings, so he poured out his heart to him, and a deep bond of love developed between them.

Chris was in tears when Brian and Jennifer came up to him. Brain put his arm around his son.

"You shouldn't have run up to him; you frightened him away. He is out in the wilds now."

"But I wanted to go with him," Chris cried.

"We can find him again, don't worry. He hasn't reached his destination yet." Brian was so relieved that they had seen Sam at last, and now he knew for sure it was the sheep that Silver was following. "He looked so beautiful standing there in the meadow, and so..." Jennifer paused for a minute trying to choose words to describe her feelings, then said "mysterious." She turned and looked at Brian with a look of wonder on her face. "He is mysterious, isn't he?" Something about the ram had given her the feeling that he had come to see if they were all right after the slide. She wondered if there was a symbolic connection in his coming to the ranch when Chris was born, and now to see if Chris was all right. It gave her an eerie feeling, and for the first time she had some understanding of Chris and Brian's need to follow him.

Brian saw the awakening interest in Jennifer's face. He recalled how thrilled she had been at the sight of the waterfall, how it cast a spell on her. His heart lifted.

"He's been a mystery to us ever since he came to the ranch," he said with hope sounding in his voice. Chris interrupted with, "Let's get going so we can catch up to him." And for the first time there was no rancor in his voice.

Chris climbed on Jingle and started riding across the meadow in the direction the ram had taken. Jennifer moved toward her horse and felt a cool breeze blowing from the icy peaks above them, and noticed for the first time that the sun had gone behind some clouds.

"What do you think the weather is up to? It's getting cold."

"It can change very quickly up here from one minute to the next, or one valley to the next. The sun is probably still shining over the ridge."

"I hope so. I'm not looking forward to sleeping in a tent

tonight if it gets much colder," she said unconvincingly. Brian laughed, "I'll keep you warm."

"In the next sleeping bag?" she asked, with laughter in her voice.

"We can zipper them together, you know. People sleep out under the stars in colder weather than this." Brian was pleased that she had laughed; she hadn't done much of it since they left home, and he loved the sound. It had the same beautiful tone as when she sang.

"Not me," she said coyly.

"You really are a Vancouver softie, aren't you? We'll have to toughen you up a bit." Brian loved to tease, and was enjoying it now; this was more what he had hoped the trip would be.

"Starting when? If there is more to toughening up than what I've already been through, I'm not interested."

"Starting right now; now get on that horse and let's go find the sun." His eyes were shining as he gave her a pat on her sore behind.

"I thought it was a sheep we were looking for," she said triumphantly.

"Okay, you win." Brian swung his leg over Glory and followed Jennifer across the meadow, after Chris who was disappearing into the bush.

10   Following the Leader

Jennifer wasn't bouncing up and down in the saddle any more. She had caught on to the knack of posting (rising out of and settling back into the saddle in time with the horse) by watching Chris and Brian. But the horse still had the best of her, and she suspected that after letting Bess have her own way like she did, it was going to be even harder to get her to obey. But obey she would, or else. Jennifer swore under her breath, as she was tired of being made a fool of by a horse. She was glad to be out of the narrow valley which confined the waters of Glenogle Creek. She preferred riding in the high open spaces like the one they were in where the jackpines were small and sparse enough for them to pass. In some places they grew so thick they posed an impassable barrier to the riders. Brian said they usually grew that way where there had once been a fire.

The clouds overhead were becoming darker, and the breeze was getting stronger as they rode along the ridge and came to a gap between the mountains that gave them a good view of the terrain ahead. Chris wanted to stop and look for Sam, and Brian said it was a good place to maybe catch sight of him again. They stopped the horses to study the terrain, and Brian designated them each an area to scan. Brian was looking over a rocky bluff to the right of the ridge they were on, and after a few minutes he yelled, "There he is, Chris!" He moved his horse over beside Christopher's and pointed to the bluff.

"Where?" Chris asked, in anxiety, fearing Sam would move before he saw him.

"There." Brian moved closer to him while pointing his finger towards the bluff. Chris was quiet for a time anxiously searching the cliff, then he almost shouted in excitement.

"I see him! I see Sam, and he is looking at us! Does he know we are coming, do you think?"

"He probably does, knowing him; he is one smart sheep."

"Oh boy! Jennifer, we found Sam, and he knows we're coming with him, look!" He was pointing in the direction of the cliff. In his excitement he had included Jennifer. He wasn't mad at her any more since she had saved him at the slide, and also found Sam. There was still a chance that Sam wouldn't reach his destination that day, and she might stay where they camped that night.

Jennifer looked in the direction Chris was pointing and saw the sheep standing on the rocky bluff looking in their direction. She had the same eerie feeling that she had experienced when she saw him in the meadow, but this time he piqued her love of mystery even more.

Even at that distance, it seemed to her that his eyes were questioning her sincerity and felt a stab of guilt at her thoughts towards Chris. She sat in speechless wonder at the power he portrayed until he turned and ambled down off the cliff and headed up the creek that ran down the bottom of the ravine. A chill wind blew, so Jennifer zipped her jacket up to her chin, and they were on their way down the bank to the creek in pursuit of Sam.

Christopher and Jingle got along fine. Jingle was a sure-footed little pony who picked his way carefully over the rough terrain with little guidance. He was used to Silver at his heels and Chris on his back.

Christopher was able to think about things. On his first day of school he met Kevin and learned that he had moved with his family from Kamloops to the ranch next to Windsong. Jennifer had taken Chris to school, as his father had already gone to the

High School where he taught. Jennifer had said she wanted to take him.

After Jennifer had left, he and Kevin were both climbing on the bars during recess when Kevin asked, "Was that your mother that came with you to school?"

Chris didn't quite know how to explain things so he said, "That's my mom. My mother went to heaven."

"Where's heaven?"

"I don't know."

"Does she live there?"

"I guess so."

"Oh, she'll come back. My mother did. She even took my baby sister and went all the way to Revelstoke and stayed with Grandma when she and my Dad had a fight." But Chris didn't think Dad and Mommy had a fight, because they didn't fight, ever. He thought it was something he had done that made her go away. He didn't know what it was he had done, but he wanted to tell her he was sorry and ask her to forgive him. He thought of Mommy every time he looked at Sam. They went together because she loved Sam so much. She took Chris out to see what Sam was doing around Windsong every chance she got. When his Dad came home they told him what Sam had been up to and they would all laugh and have a nice time together.

Chris missed those happy times when Dad sat in the family room drinking a beer while Mommy made dinner. He could go from getting goodies from Mommy to sips of beer from Dad while they talked, usually about Sam.

Sam did funny things and that meant he could join in the conversation and they would all laugh together. He liked it when they laughed. There was something magical about Sam coming to the ranch on the day he was born; he was sure Mommy thought there was.

Chris and Kevin had become friends from the first day of school, and Chris had done quite a bit of confiding in Kevin. But he hadn't told him about Sam until Kevin got bragging about going camping in their camper for the long weekend, and he was sorry about that. He hadn't told him about where Sam went or what he planned to do when they got there. Then he

112

started wondering how big heaven was, if it was small like Golden, or big like Vancouver where his Grandma Forbes lived. The riders reached the bottom of the ravine and rode along the bank of Porcupine Creek for a time, until Silver, whom they were following, got excited and started running back and forth along the bank of the creek in confusion. Brian remarked that the dog had lost Sam's tracks which meant he must have crossed the creek.

The dog came to that conclusion about the same time as Brian did, and bounded across the creek in pursuit of the sheep, and the riders followed.

The creek bed was wide and shallow and had a sand bar on the far side. Brian and Chris had already reached the bank and were waiting for Jennifer when her horse stepped on the sand bar and went down. Jennifer thought Bess had stumbled as she jumped free in time to keep from having a leg pinned under the horse. She was very shaken by the accident until she saw that Bess was about to take a leisurely roll in the sand, and it was no accident. Jennifer was furious and with the intense fury that follows a scare, she grabbed the reins and gave them a mighty jerk that brought Bess back to her feet in a hurry. Then, in the same furious state, Jennifer climbed back into the saddle and gave Bess a hearty swat on the rump with the reins. The horse trotted smartly to where Brian and Chris, who had stopped their horses to wait for Jennifer, sat watching the drama unfold in wide-eyed amazement. They were too shocked at the scene they had witnessed to speak, but eyed their riding companion with a new mark of respect.

As he turned his horse to ride along the east side of Porcupine Creek, Brian said, grinning at Jennifer, "I think you just won yourself an obedient horse, congratulations."

"Thank you," Jennifer said with a smile, as she had acted purely by instinct in her state of fury at the horse, rather than any knowledge of how to handle the animal.

After they left the ravine and Porcupine Creek they rode along the side of a mountain that was like a knoll compared to the ones around it. They were on a gentle slope with very little vegetation, making it possible for them to ride close enough to carry on a conversation. Christopher was the first to speak. He was more relaxed now that they had seen the sheep again, and was confident that his precious Sam was just a short way ahead.

"Tell us some more stories about Uncle Royd, Dad."

"I already told you all I know about him."

"But I want to hear more; tell it again," Chris said, coaxing.

"All right, I'll tell you about Uncle Albin."

"Uncle Albin?" Jennifer laughed. "Where are you getting all these uncles anyway? I thought your father only had two brothers. Or is this another great-uncle?"

"He did, but my mother had five brothers, and Albin was one of them. All right?"

"All right, I was getting a little suspicious about all these uncles you are digging up for your stories, that's all."

Brian hadn't told her much about his mother or her family other than that she died of cancer when he was 18 and that he had already gone away to university when his father remarried.

"Dad, tell the story." Chris liked it when Dad told stories about his relatives. It gave him a feeling of security, belonging to a big family. It helped him forget how unhappy he was when Mommy left and he and Dad were all alone at Windsong.

"Uncle Albin was a forest ranger and owned a number of horses, so he also did some guiding for big game hunters around Canal Flats in the years following the Second World War, when he came home from the Air Force. He had some really strange experiences, both funny and hair-raising, but this one was funny. One time Albin was to take a larger group of hunters than usual, so he asked his friend Jake, who also did a bit of guiding, to go along to give him a hand.

"The sportsmen were all prominent businessmen from Seattle. Most of them had never hunted anything bigger than a rabbit, except for their friend Lewis, know-it-all Lewis, Albin called him. He had been big game hunting around Canal Flats the year before, and unknown to Albin at the time, the guide refused to take him again.

"Lewis arranged the trip. He was a smart-aleck, that's more of Albin's description, who wanted to show off to his friends how much he knew about hunting and horses and the wilds.

Until Albin and Jake, as well as his friends, were tired of having him try to run everything. If they chose one place to camp, he knew of a better place. He insisted on doing things like saddle up the horses or pack up the pack horses, and he did it all wrong. Even around the campfire at night he did so much bragging about the last trip he was on, the others couldn't get a word in. He bragged about the size of the animals he had shot and the size of the horns he let his companions take home for trophies."

"He sounds like a winner; what did they do with him?" Jennifer asked.

"You are catching on to the ways of the wilds." Brian sounded amused. "Anyway, this Lewis got so bad he had to be put in his place. Albin and Jake got their heads together and did some scheming. Jake had been in the area the week before, and saw a bees' nest in a clump of bushes. Jake and Albin had a good time planning how to fix smart-aleck Lewis, over a bottle of rye the last night out, while alone in their tent. The friends caught on that Jake and Albin were up to something as soon as they said there was a huge elk in a clearing beyond a clump of bush they were approaching, and asked Lewis if he would like to be the one to bag it. Of course, Lewis said he would, so he rode ahead into the bush while the others sat on their horses and waited.

"When Lewis hit the bush, the bees hit Lewis and his horse spooked. Lewis let out a yell and some curses, while the horse took off at a gallop, giving smart aleck Lewis the ride of his life. When he got his horse stopped and joined the others, they told him he had frightened the elk so none of them got a shot at it. They never found out how many bees stung Lewis, as he was quiet for the rest of the trip, but the other's couldn't hide their grins when they looked at his comically swollen face."

"They were mean," Jennifer said.

"They were not mean. The guy had it coming, and they had a different sense of humor, that's all," Brian explained.

"Which you understand," Jennifer suggested.

"Yes, which I understand, don't you?" Brian was amused

every time he told the story, and it showed on his face and in his voice.

"I'm learning," she answered.

"Good for Uncle Albin, that Lewis man deserved it." Chris was agreeing with his father whether he understood the story or not.

The clouds were sinking lower in an ominous threat. It was getting darker and a chilly wind was starting to blow. A blanket of clouds had hidden the sun and robbed the earth of its warmth. Its brilliance was gone from the mountains, and the darkness that shadowed the rocks and the trees and the water robbed them of their glory.

A sound rang out that Jennifer thought at first was the backfiring of a car, and then knew it couldn't be, not in the mountains. They were a long way from the railroad and the Trans-Canada Highway, she was sure. The sound echoed and re-echoed off rocks and cliffs as it travelled through the mountains.

"What was that?" Jennifer asked in alarm as she saw Brian bring his horse to a stop with a start.

"It was a shot. Somebody fired a rifle," Brian said, anxiety sounding in his voice.

"Did somebody shoot at Sam?" Christopher asked in a voice hoarse with fear.

"No, I think it was further away than that." Brian tried to sound more confident than he felt. That someone would shoot the sheep in hunting season had been his fear every fall. He didn't even feel the sheep was safe at the ranch in hunting season.

"But we haven't seen Sam for a long time." Chris was almost tearful.

"The shot was quite a ways off, and I'm sure Sam is just up ahead," Brian said.

Jennifer sensed the uncertainty in Brian's voice, and when she saw the worried look on his face, she became concerned that it possibly was the ram some body was shooting at.

"Jennifer, maybe you and Chris should wait here for a few minutes while I ride on ahead and see what is going on."

"No, I'm not staying here; I'm going with you," Chris said, sounding anxious.

Jennifer was afraid to let Brian out of her sight after the near tragedy they had experienced the last time he left them to ride on ahead and the slide came, but if something had happened to the sheep, it wouldn't be a sight for Chris to see. She would be upset too if anything happened to Sam since she had experienced the strange encounters with him in the meadow and on the cliff, when she felt he was judging her and protecting Chris. She really was frightened of staying alone in the wilderness with Chris after the encounter with the bear the day before, and now someone with a gun was around. But she nodded her head in agreement and let Brian go.

Chris had become very upset at the thought of anything happening to Sam, and his heart was pounding so hard he could hardly breathe. Now that they had seen Sam, Chris believed the ram knew they were following him. The thought of losing him and being unable to reach their mutual destination was unbearable to the boy.

"No, I want to go. I don't want to stay here."

"You're staying here." Brian had finality in his voice for a change and didn't give in to Chris, as he rode off and disappeared into the bush ahead.

Chris started to cry. He was still mounted on Jingle, but got down at Jennifer's suggestion that they might as well get off and wait.

Jennifer went over to a stump in front of a rock pile and sat down, while Chris wandered to the edge of the cliff to look down into the ravine below where they were riding, and the dog followed him.

Jennifer was nicely conjuring up the picture of a particularly delightful candlelit dinner she and Brian had enjoyed during their courtship days, when she heard something coming through the bush that sounded like a freight train. She was petrified. Chris heard it too and came running to where Jennifer was sitting on the stump. Silver was sidling along between the direction of the noise and Chris, ready to spring at whatever was threatening his master.

Jennifer was impressed at the protectiveness the dog showed towards Chris. She wished for a moment that she had a gun, as an enormous animal with the biggest set of antlers she had ever seen came crashing out of the bush close to where she sat, protected by the pile of rocks with Chris clasped tightly in her arms. It went down over the bank into the ravine without seeming to notice the spectators. The animal looked harmless when they finally saw it coming through the bush. It was a beautiful creature and Jennifer felt sorry for having been so afraid.

By the time Brian returned Chris and Jennifer had regained their composure. "Dad," Chris cried, running to Brian in excitement as soon as he had dismounted. "We just saw a caribou. It was a great big one with huge antlers. "Didn't we, Jennifer?" He didn't wait for her to answer but went on with the story. "It came running by us really fast and went over the bank into the ravine."

"I'm impressed," Brian said with a grin, "Sam is up ahead safe and sound. I saw him. But every time I leave you two something happens. I'm glad this one wasn't as serious as the last could have been."

"Then you'd better stick around and protect us," Jennifer said teasingly. "Do you think that shot frightened the caribou? If that's what it was."

"Probably, and if it had antlers like you say, it would be a caribou. Chris knows his animals pretty well," Brian said.

"It was a caribou," Chris said. "I saw it real good. It was real close to us."

"I could see the boundary of the park from that ridge up ahead. We're nearly there. The Otterhead River is just in the next valley," Brian told them. "There is no hunting in the park, so we won't have to worry about any more shots being fired." Jennifer felt safer at the thought of traveling in a national park, and then wondered what was so much safer about the park. After all, there were wild animals there too, and she wasn't going to fall into the trap that many people do, of thinking that the animals are tame because they are in a park. She knew the parks were developed and maintained, so she asked, "Are there still wardens in the park at this time of year?"

"Could be, but I think they have probably finished getting things ready for winter. I'm not sure," Brian said.

"They might be counting the bears. Grandpa said they count the bears and things in this park." Chris sounded like an authority on such things.

"Yoho National Park, what an unusual name. It's almost like something you would call out, 'Oh Yo-ho.' What exactly does it mean, I wonder. Do you happen to know, Brian?"

Jennifer was starting to take an interest in their surroundings, and Brian was pleased, and his hopes rose again that she would learn to enjoy their way of life.

"I think the park got its name from the Cree Indian word expressing awe, yoho—wonder or astonishment, at least that's what I've always been told. But in English it means 'a call,'" Brian said.

"A call, that's beautiful." Then she laughed and said, "Well, it certainly seems to be calling Sam, and us too for that matter. It's getting cold sitting here. We may as well get moving." Jennifer walked over to Bess and prepared to mount. She felt a drop of moisture on her cheek. "I think I just felt a drop of rain."

"More like snow." Brian looked up at the darkening clouds overhead, unconcerned.

"Snow," Jennifer said, sounding alarmed.

"A little snow isn't going to hurt us. We've got lots of warm clothes," Brian informed her.

Jennifer was starting to enjoy being out in the mountains since she had acquired the knack of riding and had control of her horse. She was fascinated by the sheep and wanted to find out where he went, and what he was doing at the ranch, but the thought of being out there in the snow with just a little tent for protection in her condition unnerved her. She suspected that men become so affected by the ways of nature when they get out in the hills that they lose their sense of proportion. Although she was starting to be deeply affected by the environment, she had not lost track of common sense completely, she

119

thought; so she asked, "Brian, how do we know how far Sam is going? He could keep going like this for a week for all we know, couldn't he?"

"I don't think he is going much further. He seems to be slowing his pace like he is looking for something, probably the herd."

Brian and Chris were mounted and riding in the direction of the park, so Jennifer had no choice but to follow.

"All right, I guess you know what you're doing," she said resignedly, hoping he was wrong about the snow.

They came out of the bush onto the ridge that Brian had mentioned when he rode ahead to check on the sheep after the shot. The boundary to Yoho National Park was just below them, and beyond they could see the Otterhead River snaking through the valley. It was a beautiful sight, and Jennifer wished the sun would come out so that they could enjoy the view to its fullest. Looking at the clouds overhead she knew there was no hope of seeing the sun again that day. They rode down the bank and crossed the seven foot wide slash that marked the boundary of the park, and the thought of cutting the swath and maintaining the area the park covered on the map was mind-boggling to Jennifer. She felt safer now that they were actually in the park, and was curious about a shot being so close to it. "Brian, you didn't tell us if you found out what the shot was."

"It's hunting season, and people have a right to hunt outside the park, but not in it, but then there are people who break the law, you know." Brian hadn't liked the shot even after he found that Sam was safe. They were in a national park, and he shouldn't be carrying a firearm. A shot so close to the park could bring a warden out to investigate, and he would be in an embarrassing position. There was a chance that it was a warden destroying an animal from necessity.

On the other hand, there were hunters who broke the law and went into the park to hunt; so Sam was not entirely safe, nor were they, since hunters like that were often trigger-happy ones who shot whenever they heard something move, without waiting to identify it. Brian nudged his horse to go faster instinctively. He wanted to get deeper into the park where there was less chance of finding a foolhardy hunter on the prowl.

Jennifer felt like talking. "Brian, how far is it to the Great Divide? It fascinates me. I know you said it was the border between the two provinces."

"Yeah. It's really interesting, but it's much too far for us to ride there this time. Sometime when we drive to Calgary, I'll show you where the creek divides in half, and half of the water from that little creek ends up, as does most of the water on the east side of the divide, in the Atlantic Ocean, or the Gulf of Mexico. And that half of the creek which runs west of the divide drains into the Pacific."

"Yes, and there are some mighty rivers in the west, like the Columbia, the Fraser, and the Colorado," Jennifer was enthused.

"It's amazing when you think of how close the Columbia starts to the Kootenay, and the Columbia flows north first and makes that big bend, then turns and goes all the way down through Washington and Oregon before reaching the sea. When we go to Fort Steele and Radium Hot Springs next year, we can stop at Canal Flats and I will show you where they dug the canal in the old steamboat days so they could go from the Columbia to the Kootenay down to Billings and Libby, Montana. The Columbia River is just a little creek before it runs into Columbia Lake. The famous Big Bend Highway followed the Columbia along its big bend up through the Selkirks before the Rogers Pass was built. Before that, people had to ship their vehicles by freight to Revelstoke, if they were traveling to the coast, and the Big Bend Highway wasn't finished until the forties. Grandpa Cyrus told me many stories of the steamboat era and the construction of the Big Bend, but I'll save them for the long winter nights by the fire at Windsong."

"Oh, I'd love to hear about the steamboats, they're something that just fascinate me. I read everything I can find about the ones on the Mississippi. But where does the Kootenay River start?"

"It starts up in Kootenay National Park. You drive through it when you go from Radium to Banff. What we should do sometime is drive around the loop. We can go through the Kicking Horse to Lake Louise and Banff, then come back through Radium and up by Lake Windermere and Fairmont Hot Springs. There is a lot of beautiful country to see on that drive. I don't think many people realize how much park is in British Columbia, they think it's all Banff Park, but it isn't. Yoho and Kootenay Parks are both in B.C., and they are beautiful and have a lot to offer too."

They were riding along the west bank of the Otterhead River and just ahead of them was a little bluff that jutted out into the otherwise flat valley where the river flowed. Chris stopped his horse and pointed his finger at the bluff. "There's Sam, and he's looking this way; I think he sees us, don't you, Dad?"

"I think he sees us all right, and he knows we are following him, but I don't know if that pleases him or not."

"I think he is leading us somewhere. I have this strange feeling that he expects us to follow him." Jennifer spoke without fully realizing what she was saying. It just came out, so strong was the feeling that possessed her when the ram looked at her. Both Brian and Chris looked at Jennifer with a puzzled expression on their faces. It was the first time she had talked about Sam like that, or shown any interest in where he went, and they were surprised.

"I think the outdoors is having its effect on Mom," Brian said. He and Chris laughed, and Jennifer laughed with them. Every time Chris saw Sam he remembered more about his mother. He had a picture in his mind of her asking him what he wanted to name the sheep, and of her putting out grain for Sam in the pan they fed him with. He remembered her quite clearly leading Jingle around the yard at Windsong so he could ride. Also, a picture of her leaning over his bed to kiss him goodnight. He could see her smiling and recalled the scent of the shampoo in her long blonde hair. When she kissed him goodnight, her hair fell on his face and tickled his nose. It was like spun gold. She was beautiful, he knew by the pictures in the album, and when he thought of her, she seemed to be surrounded by a glow.

He thought of her as always smiling, but had the feeling that she was very angry with him once, but he couldn't recall why. His recollections of his mother and father together were happy ones. He knew Mommy was nice and had only left because he was bad. He knew that he was bad, but hadn't known that he was born bad, until he overheard Auntie Gail and Auntie Cheryl talking.

Auntie Gail had come up from Vancouver to bring Hazel to look after him. He hadn't understood everything, but they said it was bad when he was born, and that's why his mother went away. So he knew it was because of him. But when he told Mommy that he was sorry and would be good all the time, he was sure she would forgive him, and he wanted her forgiveness with all his heart. It was all he could think about any more. Besides, she loved Sam and Silver and the horses just like he did. He remembered her making cookies in the kitchen at Windsong, but many of his other recollections of her were vague, and he wasn't sure about them. When he asked his father about his mother he only told him a few things, and Chris had the feeling that his father didn't want to talk about her much, and he wondered why. Grandma Logan and Aunt Cheryl wouldn't say much either.

It was as if his mother was a mystery or something. Even Jennifer said she didn't know about his mother. She had only met her once when she was in Vancouver visiting her family. It was his Grandmother Forbes he should have asked because his mother was her daughter, but he had only learned that since he started school, and Grandma Forbes lived way off in Vancouver.

But after following Sam to his destination, he wouldn't need to ask anyone any more.

123

11   A Turn in the Weather

Brian was thinking about Sam and how over the years he had come to make Windsong his domain. The game warden and an ecologist had been at the ranch in the spring to take pictures of the sheep, and they thought he was about twelve or thirteen years old, which was the life span of most bighorn sheep.

Brian hoped that the sheep would stay at the ranch in his old age and die of natural causes, instead of dying in the mountains and never returning, leaving them to wonder what became of him. It would be easier for Chris to understand that Sam was just too old to live any more.

Brian worried every fall about Sam being up in the mountains during hunting season, but so far he had always come back in late November or early December, and rarely left during the winter with the exception of the odd excursion to the neighboring farms to bother their horses, usually in the middle of the night. The neighbors would tell Brian about Sam's visit the next day, as if he were one of the ranch animals and Brian was responsible for him.

They had been lucky with Sam all these years, if you could call it luck, for Sam had been a pest at times, and Brian hadn't always called him Sam. The other names he called him were not repeatable in polite company.

There was only one time that Sam showed any sign of being

injured, other than when he came when Chris was born. And that was when he returned one fall after he had been absent for a time, all cut up, with huge chunks of hair missing from his body. It had taken most of the winter for him to heal, and he had been a pretty subdued ram that year. Although Sam's presence at Windsong had been a nuisance at times, the Logans had come to love him dearly. Each fall when he went away they anxiously watched the bush across the clearing for him to return.

Sam had become a part of Windsong after some strange fate brought him into their lives.

The area that the riders were traveling through along the Otterhead River was covered with dense undergrowth, and their progress was slow and tedious. Because Yoho National Park is on the western flank of the Continental Divide, the high mountain peaks along the Divide catch moist air coming from the Pacific. Thus, it receives a great deal of rainfall which results in dense vegetation.

The clouds overhead were becoming darker and more threatening. The shadows of evening were descending at an early hour, hastened by the gathering storm. The wind was rising with the threat of turning colder and becoming more fierce as darkness fell.

Jennifer was feeling uneasy about where they were going to spend the night, as the wind grew stronger and the temperature dropped. Although she was anxious to follow Sam to see where he went now that he had cast his spell on her, as she put it, her first concern with the change in the weather was for their welfare, and her pregnancy. She was in unfamiliar surroundings and did not know what to expect from the elements. She was sure that Brian and Chris could endure far more cold and hardship than she could because they were used to it. Revealing her condition at this time, and spoiling the trip, would not make it the happy occasion she wanted it to be. She hoped it would not become necessary for her to do so.

She looked up into the darkening sky and felt another drop of moisture touch her cheek, and fear of the unknown touched her heart. As she periodically checked the sky she saw a snowflake fall, and then another, and another, until the air was full of big wet lakes that melted when they came into contact with the warm earth. But as they travelled further along the river, the flakes stopped melting and started to stay, first on the dry grass and the bushes, and then on the rocks. The earth itself was becoming white with snow. What if they got stuck up there in the mountains, what would they do? They only had enough food to last for two more days. Brian and Chris were riding on ahead oblivious to the falling snow. Someone had to use some common sense in this outfit, she thought; so at the risk of rejection she decided to make her thoughts known.

"Brian, don't you think it's getting a little ridiculous to continue with the weather getting so bad? If we turned around now couldn't we make it back to that little cabin where we camped last night? It would give us some protection from the storm." Her stomach turned over as she recalled the stench that had nearly knocked her over when she opened the door, but anything was better than nothing. She had heard of some pretty bad experiences of exposure on Vancouver's North Shore mountains when hikers and skiers had been lost, and the weather there was nothing compared to the Canadian Rockies, she suspected.

"We could never make it back there by dark," Brian said. "It's a good day's ride. Anyway, we are in the park now, and there are camping facilities if we can just find one. I know there is a hiking trail along the Otterhead River somewhere, so there should be a campsite of some kind."

"I don't want to go back, anyway, do you, Dad? We can see Sam nearly all the time now, and he knows we are coming with him. He likes it that we are here, doesn't he?"

"He might at that. He keeps looking back at us, anyway."

Jennifer resigned herself to whatever fate the two men and the ram were leading them into. She rode along behind Brian and Chris in the falling dusk in silence. It was getting so cold she was freezing.

Her horse seemed to go slower and slower as the snow fell and piled up on the ground making it slippery underfoot and difficult for them to make any headway in the dense growth along the river.

She looked at Silver following along behind Jingle and thought he was dragging his heels as well. But he came to life a few minutes later and turned around in his tracks in a flash. The hair on the back of his neck stood straight up, and he started to growl at something coming up behind them. They all stopped their horses and turned to look back down the trail in the direction they had come with growing apprehension. They could hear something coming through the bush. It wasn't making as much noise as the caribou that Jennifer and Chris had seen earlier. Not another bear, Jennifer hoped, and then she noticed that the horses were not acting up like they had when the bear had come. It was a great relief to them to see a single horse and rider emerge from the bush, and when he got closer to see that he wore the garb of the park wardens. He rode up beside them and stopped his horse. He looked just as surprised to see them as they were to see him.

"I'm Tom Shannon, the warden in this area." He stretched out his hand to Brian.

"Brian Logan," Brian said, giving the warden's hand a hearty shake, his gun forgotten.

"My wife Jennifer and my son Christopher, from Golden."

Tom Shannon made a motion to tip his hat to Jennifer and gave a nod of his head to Chris as he said, "Pleased to meet you, I'm sure."

"How do you do," said Jennifer, as Chris said a polite "hello" with a big smile of welcome.

Brian looked at Tom mounted on his horse and judged him to be a man of middle age, of stocky build, with broad shoulders and a thick chest. His face, what could be seen of it under his hat, was that of a man who had spent many hours out of doors. It was lined and weathered. His eyes had the quick observance of a person trained to authority. His manner was polite but firm, giving the impression of a strong adversary when placed in a compromising situation.

"What brings you people to the park at this time of year, and in this weather?" Tom asked in a stern voice.

"We didn't know we were coming to the park when we

127

started out, and it was beautiful yesterday and this morning," Brian answered.

"This storm just started. Probably a freak storm in this area." Tom's voice was still stern, as he caught sight of the gun in its case hanging on Brian's saddle. He stiffened noticeably, and his voice was one of authority as he pointed to the gun. "I'd like to check your gun if you don't mind."

"It hasn't been fired," Brian said as he handed his rifle over to Tom Shannon. "This isn't a hunting trip. I'm not a hunter, anyway. We are following a sheep."

"A sheep?" There was disbelief in the warden's voice as he sniffed the gun and looked it over, and then, satisfied that it hadn't been used, he sealed it and handed it back to Brian, who put it back in its sheath on the saddle.

"You mean one of your sheep has wandered this far? No chance of it still being alive. Some wild animal will have eaten it long ago." Shannon's voice was incredulous at the thought of these people coming all this way after a domestic animal. How on earth did they expect to find it in this wild country? He doubted their story, and scrutinized them a little closer. They certainly looked innocent enough. A man, a woman, and a child all on horseback with a pack horse and a dog. Out in the park in a November snowstorm looking for a sheep! Another first for the records, he thought. Wait until I tell the fellas about this one. They won't believe me.

Brian looked at Tom's weathered face and saw disbelief written all over it. "It's not a domestic sheep we are following, it's a wild one. If you look up there on that ridge ahead, you can see him. He is looking at us right now."

Tom still didn't believe them. He had been too many years in the park for this kind of nonsense, but he looked in the direction that Brian was pointing and after a few minutes he spotted the sheep on the ridge.

"Why, that's a bighorn ram," he said in amazement, and then in a stern voice, "there's no hunting in the Park." He was bristling with authority again.

"He's ours," Chris shouted at the mention of hunting.

128

"Yours?" Tom asked questioningly, taken aback by the harshness of the child's voice.

"He stays at our ranch most of the time," Brian explained. "He has for several years. He leaves about this time of year for a while, and Chris got the idea that we should track him to see where he goes. We have a few days off from school, and the weather was so nice that we thought it would be a good time to go riding in the hills."

"It's been a nice Indian summer for sure. This snow will probably be gone by tomorrow, and we will have more warm days." The warden was friendlier now, satisfied that the Logans' presence had been explained. They looked like very nice people and he could use a little company. "We may as well ride along together," he suggested, and rode in front of Brian to lead the way.

"Sounds like a good idea," Brian said, thinking a little company would be good for all of them.

Jennifer was greatly relieved to find they were not the only ones out in the wilderness in a snowstorm. Now that Tom Shannon sounded friendly, she spoke about her deep concern.

"Do you know where there is a campsite with some shelter where we could spend the night?"

"There's a group campsite on the hiking trail not far from the wardens' station where I'm staying. We will be meeting the hiking trail further along after we cross the river, which we'll have to do. It gets too steep to ride on this side after a bit. The hiking trail will make the going easier, and it will take us right to the campsite," Tom said.

Jennifer's fears about where they were going to camp for the night were no sooner calmed than the weather became a problem. The wind grew to such force that it hurled the icy snow into the faces of the horses and riders, and heaped it in mounds underfoot, hiding the treacherous rocks and logs over which they must stumble. Jennifer thought, this is what winter in Golden is going to be like, and had a moment's longing for Vancouver and the mild Pacific air. She was very glad that the warden had happened along. Not that she didn't trust Brian's knowledge of the territory, but this Tom Shannon had been riding around here all summer and fall probably, and knew every trail. Besides, she believed there was safety in numbers, and it was getting so dark they could hardly see where they were going.

When it started to snow in earnest the clouds became heavier, and what had been early afternoon dusk was rapidly becoming night. Brian, if he were totally honest, would have to admit that now that the matter of the gun in the park was over, he also was glad that Tom Shannon had happened along. Not that they were in any real danger; they had ample equipment for anything the winds of the Rockies could hurl at them, even if it meant sleeping out in the open. They had a little tent so had no worries. Thinking that Jennifer was probably scared to death, he decided a little conversation would be good to ease her fears, so even though it was difficult to talk with the wind blowing in their faces, he turned to Tom and asked, "Did you hear a shot a while back? It sounded like a rifle and must have been pretty close to the boundary of the park."

"That was probably me you heard. I fired a shot into the air to scare off a couple of coyotes that were chasing a wounded doe," Tom said.

"Was it wounded in the park?" Jennifer asked. She didn't like the thought of an animal being wounded and suffering.

"Yes, some people don't pay attention to regulations. I've no proof that the deer was shot in the park. She may have come in here after she was wounded, but there is no hunting of does anywhere; so whoever shot her was breaking the law, and if they did it in the park that makes it even worse. That's why I checked your rifle. Sorry if I seemed unfriendly, but that's my job," Tom said apologetically.

"Sorry I have a rifle in the park," Brian said, "I'm not a hunter, anyway."

"Never?" Tom asked.

"I did a bit when I was younger. But I lost interest in it after the ram came to our ranch to stay. He seems so like one of the family, I just couldn't bring myself to shoot anything that looked like him."

"I know what you mean." Tom nodded his head in agreement. "I'm going to have to make a report on that wounded doe, and get the game warden from Golden to go out and see if he can catch whoever did it. Know what his name is, by any chance?"

"Jim Farley, he's a good man. He's been in Golden for years; I know him quite well. I'm sure you'll find him very cooperative," Brian said.

The snow was falling thick and fast. They were protected from the fierce wind for a time by the steepness of the bank on their side of the river, but it was becoming to steep for safe passage. Tom reined in his horse and pointed to the river. "Here's where we cross, and the campsite and wardens' station are not too far from here."

Jennifer had been dreading having to cross the river as Tom said they must, but when she saw it she realized that the Otterhead could hardly be called a river at that point. It was more like a glorified creek, and nothing to be afraid of at all. But when her horse saw Tom's mount stumble on the slippery rocks on the creek bed, she became shy and would not enter the water. Jennifer kicked her in the flank and slapped her with the rein, but she just stepped around and around and would not cross the river.

Brian gave the lead rein of the pack horse to Chris to hold, and came back and led Bess across by the bridle. Nothing was said about the incident, so Jennifer decided it was either an unavoidable failure on the part of the horse, or Chris and Brian were not going to say anything in front of Tom. When she thought of the harassment she had received from the two of them the day before, she wished Tom had been along for the entire trip.

The hiking trail was right beside the river on the east bank, so they had difficulty finding it in the near total darkness that was now upon them due to the storm. Jennifer was becoming chilled to the point of shivering when Brian suggested they all get off and walk to get their circulation going, and Tom agreed. But when she dismounted and her feet touched the ground, she found her legs were so numb they could hardly hold her, so she stumbled along for a time until the circulation returned.

The hiking trail followed the river that flowed from east to west at that point, giving the steep bank on the opposite side a southern exposure. As the snow came down and landed on the trees and rocks still warm from the autumn sun, a mist arose obscuring what little visibility there was from the reflection of the snow that covered the ground. The mist rose like steam from the warm rocks and carried a penetrating chill.

All that Jennifer could hear of the conversation that was steadily going on between Brian and Tom was a drone that came to her through the howling wind. She trudged along in the deepening snow in a state of total exhaustion and thought she would drop by the wayside, but knew riding again meant she could freeze to death. As cold and hunger wracked her shaking body, her doubts of Brian's love returned, and as she sank further into a state of lethargy, she blamed him for her agony. How, she wondered, did he expect her to endure this hardship; and then she remembered that she was in this situation by her own choice.

She had insisted on coming along. How else was she to gain the love and respect from Brian and Chris she wanted so much, except by sharing their adventure? But as a picture of Joanne's smiling face flashed before her, she wondered with a sinking heart if it was, after all, Joanne who was between them all. She was frightened by the thought. How could she fight a ghost? A memory of someone so beautiful. She became unnerved at the sudden realization that she resented the picture of his mother that Chris kept in his room. She dreaded facing that serene confident girl who smiled from the golden frame every time she entered Christopher's room.

She stumbled over a rock on the path and her horse jumped and startled her. And at that moment she hated horses, and dogs, as Silver brushed past her all wet and stinking, and all animals. And, come to think of it, she even hated little boys who wanted to go off into the wilderness. Jennifer's feeling of defeat was so great that she almost wished she had stayed home, almost but not quite, because there was no way she was going to become a domestic drudge. No damn way she was going to let these two men turn her into something she abhorred. As scalding tears coursed down her icy cheeks, rebellion rose and she trudged on more determined than ever.

The men and horses came to a stop. They had arrived at the campsite, and Jennifer's heart sank into the icy pit where her stomach had once been. The place, which on a nicer day probably held nothing but intrigue, was to her, in its shroud of snow, the scene that fit a poem she once read, a desert-place of nothingness.

Brian and Tom, who had been talking non-stop, were suddenly silent as they all stood and viewed a summer campground on a winter night while the prospect of finding any comfort under such circumstances faded.

Tom looked from the desolate campground to Jennifer and saw her hastily brush a tear from her white face, but a tight withdrawn look remained. She felt Tom's scrutiny of her, and looked up to see him looking at her with compassion. At that moment she did not care that her feelings were so evident on her face that a stranger might read them. The silence lengthened until it was broken by Tom clearing his throat.

"It sure doesn't look like you would be very comfortable here. Why don't you come on up and spend the night with me at the station? The quarters are a bit small, but there are four bunks."

He was watching Jennifer's face while he spoke, a look of concern on his own, and when she nearly smiled he continued jokingly, "I only snore loud enough to lift the roof off."

They all laughed.

"Thanks, Tom. That would be great," Brian accepted, after looking at Jennifer who nodded her head in approval. He wouldn't mind spending the night in the tent despite the weather, nor would Chris, he knew. Another time, perhaps, he thought. He realized that Jennifer was near exhaustion, and doubted if she would ever come again, but suddenly he knew he would miss her if she didn't.

"The station's not much further up the trail, and I think we'd better keep on walking; we can keep warmer that way. I was caught out here in a snowstorm once that was so bad I couldn't see a thing. I had to let my horse lead me home," Tom said as they continued up the hiking trail leading their horses, while the snow swirled around them and the darkness deepened.

"You must have had some interesting experiences being a park warden," Brian commented, pleased at the thought of spending the evening with Tom and spinning a few tales. He was about to ask Tom how long he had been a warden when a gust of wind hit them with such force they had to lean into it to keep their balance. They quickened their steps as the need to reach the wardens' station became pressing.

12   Flood of Memories

Chris was quietly trudging through the snow trying to keep pace with his father and Tom, after he had told Tom in no uncertain terms that Sam was theirs. The snow reminded him of Christmas as there was always snow at Windsong at that special time of year.

He had gone with his mother and father to the bush at the edge of the clearing on the mountain side of the ranch to get a Christmas tree. They rode out in the snowmobile, and after they had chosen the perfect tree for them to decorate, Chris sat with his mother in her snowmobile while his father went to chop the tree down. There had been a heavy fall of snow the night before and the branches were laden. His father swung his ax, which landed full force on the trunk of the tree giving it a mighty shake. The tree swayed back and forth and dumped the burden of snow from its branches onto his father's head, and a good deal of the cold snow found its way inside his Dad's shirt. Mommy roared with laughter as his Dad used some words that Chris knew were bad. "Don't you know you have to shake the tree first?" Mommy said as she doubled over with laughter, not seeing Dad scoop a handful of snow that he threw and caught her full in the face. She jumped off the snowmobile and grabbed some snow and the fight was on. Chris laughed with glee as he helped Mommy throw snow at Dad while his father teased him about being on his mother's side.

When they were exhausted from their snowball fight and the laughter that ensued, they looked up and saw that Sam had followed and was standing watching them. "Sam thinks we're silly," his father said, and then he chopped down the tree. Chris rode back to the house with Mommy while his father took the tree. It covered him and the snowmobile while the remainder trailed behind through the snow.

Many of Christopher's memories of his mother were in connection with something funny that Sam had done. Like the time his father took the truck to haul hay from the stack by the barn to the pasture in the meadow below the house, when the snow was too deep for the horses to paw through to eat the dry grass. His mother was holding him up to the window so he could watch his father as it was too cold for him to go along.

Sam liked to bury himself in the hay where he was warm and cozy and couldn't be seen. Chris watched from his mother's arms while his father walked to the truck which he had loaded with hay the night before. As he bent to close the tail-gate Sam, who was inside, came flying out while his father jumped out of the way in alarm, and stood threatening Sam with a shaking fist, while Chris and Mommy laughed at the amusing sight.

There was a picture in the album of Sam standing in hay on top of the canopy of the truck that his mother had taken. Instead of making two trips his Dad had piled hay on top of the canopy as well as filling the back of the truck, and Sam had jumped up there to be in the hay. Sam did a lot of funny things, Chris thought, smiling to himself.

Chris hardly noticed when they stopped at the campsite and decided to spend the night in the Warden's cabin with Tom. He was enjoying remembering those happy times. When his father mentioned that Sam was going slower and seemed to be looking for something, Chris knew what it was that Sam was looking for. It was what he was looking for, too, and he got very excited thinking they were nearly there. He was so carried away that he hadn't noticed how dark it was getting and that they couldn't see Sam any more. He stubbed his toe on a rock and realized if it snowed all night even Silver wouldn't be able to find Sam's tracks by morning. He was about to mention his concern to his father, but had to wait until Tom stopped talking. "I always leave a light on in the cabin when I go out since I had that scare in the snowstorm. It can get so dark in the forest without the moon or the snow for reflection, you can't see your finger in front of your face. If you're not equipped to spend the night out of doors, it can be a pretty frightening experience."

After listening to Tom, Chris realized they would soon be stopping for the night, and he wanted to speak to his father about finding Sam's tracks in the morning if it kept on snowing. He manipulated Jingle over beside Glory so that he could walk beside his father. He tried speaking to him quietly, but his father couldn't hear him in the howling wind. Tom was talking again, so Chris started pulling on his father's sleeve, a trick he had for getting his attention. He finally got Brian's attention.

"Did Sam cross the river when we did, do you think?"

"I don't know, Chris, it was too hard to see through the snow." Brian spoke with more annoyance than he usually did when speaking to his son.

"If he didn't, how are we going to find him in the morning? We shouldn't have crossed the river; we should have kept on following Sam." Chris sounded distraught.

Brian lost his patience with the child when he saw that he was becoming unreasonable about following the sheep, and said to him angrily, "We can't worry about Sam right now; we have to concern ourselves with getting out of this storm before we freeze to death." Then, seeing the hurt that came into his son's eyes, while his chin stuck out in determination, guilt added fuel to Brian's anger and he shouted at Chris, which he had never done before. "Why can't you be reasonable, God damn it; can't you see we are in an impossible situation?" When he looked at his son's face, Brian recognized the will of iron that had been in his grandfather Cyrus, and he was shaken.

They had stopped on the trail and Jennifer, who had been lagging behind, caught up to them. Chris turned on her like a panther after its prey. "If we hadn't stopped all the time so you could look at everything, we could have kept up to Sam."

Brian was so shocked at Christopher's outburst it took him a minute to find his voice, but when he did, it held a threat.

"Christopher!"

"We could too. You and me could have kept up to Sam. We could be with him right now instead of him getting lost." Chris had shouted so loud he had to stop for breath.

"Christopher, you stop that." Brian had never seen his son act like this before, and didn't know how to handle him, while Jennifer stood numbly by saying nothing. He reached out to take hold of the boy to calm him down as he had obviously lost control. But Chris stepped out of the way and burst into tears. "Now we will never find where Sam goes. I know we won't." He started crying harder. "I wish Jennifer had stayed home." Chris was hungry and tired, and now that he had given way to tears he could not stop the flow. They tumbled down his cheeks and fell onto his jacket where they were lost in the snow that gathered there.

Christopher's outburst was followed by stunned silence, while the wind increased to a wailing pitch and the swirling snow enveloped them. A creaking sound was heard above the howling wind as Tom yelled, "Look out!" They all jumped out of the way as a giant fir, which had stood in the forest for a hundred years, gave way to the forces of the wind and thundered down across the path in a heap of broken limbs. "More of them are likely to come down in this wind. We'd better hurry," Tom warned.

The gentle singing of the wind in the trees that Jennifer had heard and come to love at Windsong was nothing compared to the torrent that was tearing the whole forest apart and hurling it at them. Bits of limbs and branches were strewn across the path. She was hurt by Christopher's angry accusations, and thought he must have a deep resentment of her to have acted the way he had. If that were so, then all her hopes and dreams of a happy married life with Brian were dashed. How, she wondered, was she going to tell her husband the happy news she had been bursting to tell him for two days? The tears started down her cheeks again.

No one spoke as they trudged on in the swirling snow and darkening afternoon. Jennifer pulled the hood of her jacket across her face to protect it from the snow that felt like bits of ice hitting her full force. Her hands were cold even with her gloves, and she remembered how foolish she thought Brian was when he insisted on her taking them. That beautiful autumn day when they started out for a ride in "Brian's hills," that seemed so long ago, was only yesterday. It felt to her like they had been walking for hours. She knew she couldn't go on much longer, and was about to ask how far the cabin was when she saw a light shining through the trees and was relieved to hear Tom say in a heartening way, "The station's just ahead; you can see the light through the trees there," and he pointed eagerly ahead. They walked around a bend in the trail, and there was the Warden's Station not more than a few hundred yards away.

Jennifer could have run the distance to the cabin as she had a sudden burst of energy she never would have believed she had. She thought it must be like this when people lost in the desert suddenly find water. She had always wondered where in the movies of the old west they got that burst of energy when they were nearly dead, to run to the water after they crossed Nevada or Arizona. She had considered it a hoax of the movie makers, but knew her own burst of energy was born of extreme need.

"Well, we're here," Tom said in a hearty voice as he dropped the reins and went to open the door. It looked like pretty close quarters for the four of them to spend the night in, but at that moment Jennifer didn't care; all she wanted was to get inside out of the cold. And that is what she did, along with Christopher, as soon as the door was open, leaving Brian and Tom to tend to the horses and bring in their belongings.

She barely had time to look around the dim interior when Tom came in with an armful of wood and kindling for the fire. He turned up the lamp and then went to the stove and laid the fire, while Jennifer looked around and saw that the station was much larger than it had looked from the outside; the logs had been deceiving. As the fire started to crackle and Tom went out to help Brian with the horses, she pulled a chair up to the stove and sat down, still dressed in her heavy outdoor clothes. Chris sat on a chair on the other side of the stove but did not look at her. She wiped her face with a tissue from her pocket in case the tears had left a stain, and pushed the hood of her jacket off her head. A little smoke had escaped from the stove before Tom had it going to his satisfaction and closed the door, so the room smelled of smoke from cedar wood and pine.

She noticed the table by the wall on the far side of the room held radio equipment and was pleased to think they had contact with the outside world, after all.

The glass in the doors of the stove were red with fire and the warmth radiated into the room. Jennifer and Chris removed their jackets as Brian and Tom came in covered with snow. They made their way to the stove and stood over it while it steamed and hissed as the snow from their garments fell on the hot steel. They were both laughing at some joke they had shared before entering. Another mountain man, Jennifer thought; Tom is just like Brian. They thrive on this type of experience. They call it adventure and talk about it for years.

The kettle of water Tom had placed on the stove when he made the fire was starting to sing, and it added a note of cheer to the rustic interior of the cabin. Brian brought out a bottle of rum while Tom got mugs from the cupboard along with honey, nutmeg and butter. A couple of sips of the hot spicy drink made them more jovial than ever.

"Sure glad you happened along with this rum, Brian. I was right out of the stuff, and there is nothing like a hot rum to take the chill out of your bones, I always say. Anyhow, it gets kinda lonely out here in the mountains after a while. I don't mind it so much in the tourist season as there is always somebody around, but at this time of year I don't very often see anybody."

"I thought the park would be all closed up by now." Brian was thinking of the gun he carried into the park unintentionally. It was sealed now, but he was still feeling a little bad about it. He didn't like being on the wrong side of the law at any time, even if it was only slightly.

"We don't usually close up the stations until after hunting season unless the weather gets extremely bad. Good thing I was here, cause it looks like maybe somebody is breaking the law and hunting in the park boundaries."

Brian poured another drink for Tom and himself, and added more hot water to the one Jennifer already had when she raised her mug to the kettle he was pouring. The drink was spreading a soothing warmth through Jennifer's body, making her glad to be in the warm cabin, out of the storm. She pushed her chair back from the stove as Tom added more wood, and the delicious warmth it gave increased. Tom came over and tipped his mug to hers, and said, "Here's to you Jennifer, come on, cheer up." She really had to smile, Tom was such a jovial person, a father type, doing everything he could to make them comfortable. Things were not so bad after all.

Tom noticed Jennifer's cheeks were getting pink from the rum, but she still looked tired; a pretty girl, he thought, not used to the outdoors. I wonder what made her come along, and then she looked at Brian, and Tom had the answer.

He knew what it meant to have a girl look at you like that; he was not so old, and he envied Brian Logan. "Why don't you just sit right there, Jennifer, and soak up some heat while Brian and I make us something to eat. You look like you could use a rest. I'll bet you have been doing for these two bums ever since you left home. How long have you been on the trail?"

Jennifer smiled her most heart-warming smile at Tom after his suggestion, and propped her feet up on a stool he brought for her while Brian and Chris, who were now relaxed, laughed at Tom's reference to them as bums.

"We left home yesterday morning," Brian said. "We spent last night by that old cabin along Hospital Creek, if you know the area where that is."

"Like the back of my hand. Spent my whole life around here. I was born and raised in Field, B.C. Now what do you want for supper? I'll see if I've got it."

"We have some steaks, that's all these two want when they're riding." Jennifer made a move to get the pack with their provisions, that Brian had left against the wall, but Tom held up his hand for her to stay where she was as Brian went to the pack for their food, and Tom started peeling potatoes and slicing them into a large cast iron frying pan. Then he opened the door of his little gas refrigerator and brought out an enormous steak and said, "You're men after my own heart. There is nothing like a steak after a hard day's ride in the fresh air."

Chris noticed that Tom had included him in the "men" and smiled.

They had another drink as they were all in the mood to celebrate, it seemed. Even Chris was allowed a second few drops of rum with lots of hot water and honey, while Tom fried the potatoes and Brian broiled the steaks.

They were all so hungry when they sat down at the table that no one spoke until the meal was finished; then Jennifer proposed a toast to the chefs. She said it was the most delicious meal she had ever eaten, and meant it.

After supper they were all four around the stove with their feet up and their chairs tipped back while the wind howled around the corners of the little cabin. Jennifer was finding that life in the wilds was not so bad inside a warm cabin. It was very relaxing to sit snug and warm inside, while nature had her way with things outside.

There was a scratch at the door and Tom got up to let Silver in. The dog found his way to the stove and lay down with his front paws stretched out in front of him.

"At home he doesn't come in." Brian sounded surprised.

"He just wants to get the snow off his coat; let him stay, Dad."

"Chris has a deep insight into Silver," Brian laughed.

"Animals know when they can get away with things," Tom remarked. "What's this about that sheep you were following? You said he stays at your place."

"Yes, he came the day Chris was born. He goes away sometimes but always comes back. He leaves for the longest period this time of year."

"Sure, because it's the rutting season. You're lucky he comes back. They don't live very long, you know, when they start fighting over the ewes."

"I didn't think they usually killed each other fighting, at least not from what I've read." Brian wished he had finished his book about the mountain sheep.

"No, but they get weak and other wild animals get them." Christopher had been getting drowsy, but when Tom and his father started talking about sheep he perked up. "Mr. Shannon, do you think we will be able to find Sam tomorrow?"

"Sam?"

"That's his name."

"I saw some ewes over in the next ravine the other day. You could look there, except it's awful steep to get there."

"Can we go tomorrow, Dad?"

"I guess we'll have to if we can't find him around here. What exactly is it like, Tom, the terrain?"

"Rough, steep and rough. The kinda country that sheep go into, but if you don't mind traveling a little further, you can follow along the Otterhead until it levels off a bit, and comes back down the valley on the other side where it's not so steep."

"Can we do that, Dad?"

"We might as well. We've come this far to see where Sam goes; no use turning back now."

"Oh, good!"

Jennifer noticed that Chris was getting sleepy, but couldn't decide if she should risk another rebuff from him by suggesting bed, or wait until Brian noticed that it was getting late for him to be up. She decided she may as well take the "bull by the horns," as the saying goes, which she did. He got right up from his chair without making any fuss, said goodnight, and crawled into his sleeping bag in the top bunk, on the far side of the room where it was decided that he and Tom would sleep. He gave them all a dimpled smile, then snuggled down and turned his back to them. He must be satisfied that they would be going after Sam in the morning, Jennifer decided, or he would have rebelled, as he usually did, about being sent to bed.

Tom stoked up the fire and added wood, while Brian fixed their drinks which Jennifer declined, and settled themselves at the stove to enjoy the evening. The cabin creaked under the straining wind, and the fire in the stove crackled and spread warmth to the logs on the cabin walls.

"How does your stock accept that sheep at your place?" Tom asked.

"The ram leaves Silver alone, but he bothers the horses a lot," Brian said. "Every spring he chases the horses around for about two weeks trying to take them up into the mountains with him. When they won't go, he becomes frustrated.

"One year he chased the pony so much it nearly died of exhaustion. During the summer he usually stays up in the hills. We think he stays close to the ranch because he comes down about every three weeks to check on things. He seems to show up every time we make any changes like moving the horses to another pasture or if a strange horse comes to board." Brian stopped to take a drink from his mug.

"He sounds like quite a character," Tom said, amused. "What else does he do?"

Brian continued, "Whenever we have a female pony at Windsong, he tries to breed her every fall."

"I can understand that; the fall is the mating season for the sheep."

"The winter we had two weaning fillies, he chased them constantly; so I had to put them in a chain link fence enclosure in the yard. He was so frustrated after that, he spent hours smashing his horns against a pine tree that grows by the gate, and managed to debark several feet off the poor tree. He won't jump over a barbed wire or chain link fence, although he can jump over a six foot pole fence; he goes under barbed wire, but chain link he won't go near."

Tom laughed, "Sounds like he has his druthers, and he thinks he owns your horses, I'd say."

Brian laughed too. "He also thinks he owns us, we suspect. It's a bit unnerving to look out our kitchen window and see a mountain sheep standing there watching what is going on inside, I can tell you."

"What? That's hard to believe."

"It's true, he does that, doesn't he, Jennifer?" Brian continued without waiting for Jennifer to answer. Tom was a good listener, and he was enjoying himself.

"I have a habit of feeding the animals their grain, each in their own spot. I started giving grain to the sheep too, but he was so fond of it he expected it every time I went near his spot, it didn't matter if it was feeding time or not. He got so mad when he didn't get it that I had to stop feeding it to him altogether, or face being struck with the force behind twenty five pounds of horns. I chose to stop the grain."

"Yeah, there is a tremendous force behind those horns. He must eat hay, though, doesn't he?"

"He has access to hay any time he wants; he just goes into the hay corral and helps himself and the horses too."

"I've read Andy Russell's book, *Horns In The High Country*; it's all about guiding trips in the Rockies and there is quite a bit about wild sheep, but I had no idea they had so much character. Has this one always been like that or did he just get that way at your place?"

"He gets a little bolder all the time, but he has always been a bossy, overbearing animal. Of course, I don't have any others to compare him to. He is sure no gentleman, I can tell you. When it rains or snows, he chases the horses out of the shed and stands in there all warm and dry by himself while the horses shiver out in the cold."

Tom threw back his head and roared. "No kidding, that must make him popular with the horses."

"You should see him standing in there like a damn sultan while my horses are out in the cold. And the pattern is always the same, no matter what horses we have at the ranch. If there's an old mare, he has no use for her so they torment each other all the time. He ignores the youngest. He bullies Christopher's pony, and loves Jennifer's mare. They play games together."

"Games. That animal's incredible; what on earth kinda games do they play?"

"Here, Tom, let me touch up your drink first." Brian looked at Jennifer, but she shook her head. no, so he fixed one for himself and Tom and sat down again by the stove.

"They play chicken, I call it. They both rear up on their

hind legs and charge towards each other, then veer off at the last minute. I have also seen them standing nose to nose, and they chase each other around the pond down in the meadow pasture."

"Have you taken pictures of them doing some of this stuff?" Tom asked, incredulous.

"We've got hundreds of pictures of him. I've never really told anyone about him before as we don't want word to get around that he is there."

"I don't blame you for that; people can be pretty thoughtless, especially at hunting season. Sounds to me like Sam — is that what Chris calls him?"

"Yes, he named him Sam when he was so small that's about the only name he knew."

"It sounds to me like Sam thinks it's mating season all year long at your ranch. The rams only meet with the ewes once a year, you know. I'll say one thing for him, he's not dumb." Tom was enjoying himself.

"No, he's not dumb. When he can't get at the horses, he gets frustrated and beats his horns against whatever shrub or brush that's close, like a spoilt child. We looked after a neighbor's female goat once. She came into heat at our place and Sam fell madly in love with her. He wouldn't leave her alone; so I had to put her in a pen with a page wire fence, and he tried to smash the fence down with his horns by ramming and smashing against the posts. That was in December and the goat had a miscarriage in January, but they never found the fetus. The veterinarian in Golden said it was possible for Sam to have bred her."

"That's hard to believe, you know, that a wild animal would live at your ranch like that. Incredible. Chris is obsessed with him, too. Sure hope nothing ever happens to him."

"He gets tamer every year and it worries me. At first he used to take off for the woods every time a strange vehicle drove into the yard, but now he just sticks around to see what's going on." He paused, and then said, "Let's hear some of your experiences, Tom. You must have had some good ones being a park ranger. Here, I'll sweeten up our drinks first." Brian got up and did the honors, while Tom filled the stove.

Jennifer handed her mug to Brian for a refill after the effects of the first one wore off. She was relieved that things between her and Chris were back to normal, or she hoped they were. She was enjoying sitting by the fire listening to the conversation between Tom and Brian.

Tom was revelling in all his experiences as a park warden over the years and Brian was taking it all in. She grew a bit drowsy listening to the men's conversation, and her mind drifted off to other things. She started thinking about her relationship with Gail, and was sorry that even though it was better, it was not the great one it had been in the past, and she missed it.

One of the pleasant aspects of marrying into the Logan family was that she and Gail would be sisters-in-law, they jokingly said, which of course they wouldn't be. But it had been a pleasant thought that they would somehow be closer; instead, as it turned out, they were further apart. Jennifer blamed Gail for the rift. It had seemed to her that Gail wanted to control Brian's life and that she, Jennifer, could only have him or the two of them as much as Gail wanted her to and no more. That was when she rebelled, and told Gail that she and Brian were getting married, and he would be hers from then on. She had gone to Gail's for coffee, all excited about telling her that she and Brian were getting married. They had been seated at the nook looking out at the garden and the green belt beyond, when Gail asked, "How's the big romance coming?"

Something in the tone of Gail's question irritated Jennifer. She became annoyed at Brian and Gail discussing their relationship. She had started feeling that their seeing each other, where they went and what they talked about was private; so she said, "Haven't you talked to Brian?"

"No, I haven't seen him lately and he wasn't home last night when I called. Mom said he was with you and that Chris was home with her. I didn't know you were going out last night. Where did you go?"

Jennifer was piqued at the tone in Gail's voice and felt that she was prying into her affairs. She hadn't minded telling Gail about it before it became serious and she had discovered she was in love with Brian. Since then she resented Gail's inquisitiveness. She wanted to tell her that they were getting married and for them to be happy about it together, instead of being questioned about private details; so she answered her with resentment, "I don't think it's any of your business." She didn't mean to say that; it just came out.

"Aren't you forgetting that he's my brother-in-law?" Gail's face was flushed with anger.

"He won't be much longer, we're getting married."

"I don't appreciate the tone of voice you're using. You seem to have forgotten who introduced you." Gail had become very upset when Jennifer mentioned marriage.

"You have been running Brian's life, but from now on you will have to deal with me."

"Deal with you. Who do you think you are? This is my sister's husband and son you are talking about, and you don't get the right to own them just like that. You'll find out."

At that point Jennifer became so upset she couldn't speak without letting go the flood of tears that was welling up inside her; so she got up from the nook and ran out of the house to her car, and drove home crying all the way. Jennifer was afraid she would lose Brian, but when she told him that evening, he said not to worry about Gail. She hadn't seen her again until after they had their quiet wedding, and came back from their honeymoon at the Shuswap Lakes.

She recalled how nervous she had been meeting Gail again. Chris had gone to the cottage with the Forbes, and she and Brian went down for the day to pick him up. Everyone was at the beach when they arrived, Gail and Alex, her sister Lynn and her husband Doug, and Madeline. Madeline completely ignored their rift and carried on as if nothing had happened. She wasn't going to have any problems in her family, that was obvious, nor was she going to let go of Brian, whom she loved like a son, or of Chris, her firstborn grandson, Jennifer could see. She certainly was a strong lady, and Jennifer had a great deal of respect for her. She felt that Madeline had put her trust in her to look after Brian and Chris and that she genuinely wanted all three of them to be happy. Jennifer did not want to fail and break that trust. She was determined not to, and this business of Chris rejecting her had to be worked out somehow.

She had been happy and proud when Chris called her Mom, until he started asking Brian to track Sam. It seemed that he changed afterwards. He was so like the Logans, quiet and reserved, and hard to reach.

Jennifer had never known people like the Logans and the Forbes. Although Brian and Jennifer were married, there was still a strong bond between Brian and the Forbes family. Jennifer was beginning to feel that the tragedy of Joanne's illness and death was encompassing both families, and Brian and Chris were at the core of it. She would have to break through that wall in order that she, Brian and Chris could live their own lives. Joanne Logan had been on her mind lately. She met her once at the Forbes when Joanne came to Vancouver with baby Chris to visit her parents. She liked Joanne right away and thought she was a lovely person. Little did she dream at the time that she would one day be trying to raise the son Joanne was hugging to her breast.

She wondered what Brian had told Chris about his mother's death; not very much, she suspected, as she recalled the questions Chris started asking when she first came to Windsong.

Jennifer had been hanging some clothes in the closet and Chris was sitting on the bed watching her. She looked lovingly at a blue dress she had worn to dinner when she and Brian became engaged, and wondered if she would ever have an opportunity to wear it in Golden.

"My Dad sold my mother's clothes, you know," Chris said emphatically. "I'm sure he didn't, Chris," she said. Then seeing that he was watching her intently, apprehensive irritation rose in her, as this was not the first time he had confronted her with questions of this nature, and the tone of his questioning was becoming more demanding each time.

"What did he do with them, then?"

"I don't know exactly, but he probably gave them to the needy." At first she thought he was like a shrewd lawyer trying

149

to solve a mystery, and then she wondered if it was Christopher's way of reminding her that she was not the first. She was reminded of the shadow she felt lurking in the corners and watching, and was filled with dread.

"Doesn't she need them?"

"No, Chris, she doesn't."

"He sold her car; why did he sell her car?"

"Because he didn't need it."

He was silent for a few minutes watching her.

She tried not to show her uneasiness and to think of a way to distract him from his questioning.

"My mother took all those pictures in the album."

"I know she did."

"Why did she take them?"

"She liked to, it was her hobby." She was becoming more exasperated as she didn't like being reminded of the happy times Brian had shared with Joanne.

"Dad said she was good at it, and people asked her to take pictures at their weddings too. Did you know that?" He pulled a picture of Sam from his pocket and added, "Isn't it good? I'm keeping it for her."

"It's very good. Look, why don't we go for a walk down to the pond in the meadow?"

"So I can catch frogs?" he asked, all smiles.

"All right," she said resignedly, not being crazy about frogs.

Jennifer had evaded the questions as best she could until such a time as she could bring herself to broach the subject with Brian, but once Chris became obsessed with following Sam, and developed a resentment towards her, he stopped asking questions about his mother. However, the questions he did ask bothered her. They made her suspect that the reality of his mother's death had not been explained to Chris, and that he hadn't understood.

The more she thought about it the more she felt that there was some mystery surrounding Joanne, but she didn't know what. And she suspected it was something she wasn't allowed to share. She was also starting to feel that this mystery was the shadow between the three of them. Jennifer believed that if Chris loved her, Brian would stop worrying about Chris and would allow himself to love her too.

Her thoughts were interrupted by a roar of laughter from the two men as they sat by the stove telling tall tales while the line of dark liquid in the rum bottle came closer to the bottom.

Tom filled the stove with wood as Brian went to fill the mugs, but Tom raised his hand and said, "No more for me thanks, I've had enough."

"Are you sure? There's not much left." Brian held up the bottle to show Tom. "There's just enough for a couple more, we may as well kill it."

"Give it to Jennifer; she hasn't had very much. It'll make her sleep well and she won't hear that howling wind."

"Jennifer, will you help me kill this off?"

"All right, I'll have a nightcap with you."

When Brian handed her a mug of rum and sat down again himself, they were quiet, and the ticking of Tom's clock on the cabin wall drew her attention. "It's not that late; the evening has seemed so long I thought it would be later than that," she said.

"No, but it's my bedtime," Tom said as he made a motion to get up. "So if you will excuse me I think I'll turn in."

"Will we disturb you if we sit here a while and finish our drinks?" Jennifer asked.

"Not the way I sleep, that wind could tear the roof off and I wouldn't know it." Tom got up and went over to the bunk in the corner where Chris was sleeping as they said goodnight.

Brian and Jennifer sat quietly for a time after Tom left while the wind howled around the cabin with such force it sounded at times as though it would indeed take the roof off. The fire crackled and sparked in the stove and sent whiffs of smoke through the doors into the room when the wind found its way down the chimney. The clock on the wall ticked away the evening hours. Chris lay listening to his dad telling Tom all the funny things that Sam had done. He thought for a time about how important it was to find Sam in the morning so he could follow him to their destination.

Then he thought about his mother as he always did when thinking of Sam. Dad gave Mommy a movie camera for her birthday and she was trying it out in the yard. She wanted to get some movies of Sam, she said, so Chris was to run beside Sam while Mommy experimented with her camera. She said things to make him laugh as he followed Sam around the yard. It was a happy day and he could relive it when Dad showed the movies to him and he could feel close to Mommy too, but they hadn't looked at the movies for a long time, and he missed seeing them. He thought again of his need to tell her he was sorry that he was bad, and ask her to forgive him.

In a state of sleep and wakefulness he imagined that he was at the peak of the mountain. The sun was shining and the grass was all green. Sam was running ahead of him and he was running to catch up to Sam. He looked up and saw a soft white cloud at the top of the mountain, and his mother was there. Sam started running faster and he started running faster too. Soon he was running as fast as he could, but he still could not catch Sam. So he started calling out to him, "wait for me, Sam, wait for me," but Sam just kept right on going until he reached his mother, and she put out her arms to Sam and they went together up into the cloud at the top of the mountain and disappeared without waiting for him. He called and called, but they were gone. There was only the sunshine, and the green grass, and the white cloud. Chris twisted in his sleeping bag and sobbed in his sleep. When he awoke in the morning, he was more determined than ever to find Sam.

It wasn't long until Tom was sleeping, and true to what he told them his snoring was giving competition to the wind in its effect to remove the roof. Brian and Jennifer looked at each other and smiled.

"If anything keeps us awake tonight it won't be the wind," Jennifer said as she leaned back in her chair and pushed the stool closer to the stove with her foot until she was almost in a reclining position. This was the first time she had been alone with Brian since they had left home except for the few minutes they had spent by the campfire.

The evening's conversation with Tom had been good for

Brian, she thought. He looked more relaxed than he had looked for weeks. She was thinking how happy he would be when she told him about the baby. Then Brian spoke.

"I sure hope it stops snowing by morning so we can find where Sam went."

"Are you planning on looking in that ravine Tom mentioned?" Jennifer asked, while all thoughts of telling him about the baby vanished as she saw that he was totally occupied with the problems at hand. He wasn't ready.

"Yes, Chris will insist that we go there if we can't find him around here."

"Why do you think he is so determined to find where Sam goes? It's almost like a fever with him."

"I don't know, that's what I want to find out. He loves him a lot, I guess," Brian said, sounding puzzled.

"Joanne loved Sam too, didn't she?"

Brian gave her a questioning look, then said in a soft voice, "Yes, she did. Yes, she loved Sam very much. She felt there was some meaning in his coming to Windsong when Chris was born. I can still see him standing by the corral the day I brought them home from the hospital, with that gash in his chest still open and raw looking. I told Joanne he was there, and she couldn't wait to come home and see him. .

"She got out of the car and walked towards him, and he just stood there as if he was expecting her, and she said, 'Bring Christopher to me,' but when I put the baby in her arms, Sam started moving away; so I retreated and he came within a few feet of Joanne and Chris and stood there looking at them. It was as if some message was passed between those three. It was uncanny," Brian continued as if Jennifer was not there. "She just seemed to have communication with animals as if she understood how it was for them, and they knew it."

"With people too, they tell me," Jennifer said.

"Yes," Brian said wonderingly, "with people too."

"Did Christopher go to her funeral?"

"No, oh God no, how could he go to her funeral?" Brian's voice had become an anguished whisper. He was leaning forward with his elbows on his knees, and he covered his face with his hands.

"Why not?" she asked gently. "Children do go to funerals of their parents, you know, so they can understand."

"No, it was too terrible; no, he couldn't go."

"But you knew she was going to die, didn't you? I mean, she was sick."

He looked at her then, and the pain she saw in his eyes was so intense she reached out her hand to him and he took it in his own. Time hung between them, while the clock on the wall ticked away, and Brian sank into the agony of recalling the past.

"She didn't have to die. She only wanted to." His voice became choked with tears.

"What?" Jennifer asked incredulously, as fear of what he was about to say gripped her heart.

"She took her own life." He paused, looking at her for understanding. "Didn't you know that?" And tears welled up in his eyes.

"No, no, I didn't know, oh my God." She was on her knees beside him, her arms around his shaking shoulders, and her head pressed to his.

"I'm sorry, how terrible it must have been for you, for all of you." Understanding flooded her heart for the first time. And she said, "No wonder, no wonder." She drew back and looked into his eyes. "Don't blame yourself, don't blame yourself." But she saw that nothing could release Brian from the secret chambers of torment; so she sat hunched on the floor with her arms around his neck and felt the tears of pent up pain running down his face and onto hers.

"She left Chris with my sister, and went to a motel." His voice was so choked up he could say no more, and then he gained enough control to say, "She took an overdose of her medication."

They sat huddled together in silence for a long time. And after he calmed down she kissed him and whispered, "You can't keep on suffering like this; it wasn't your fault."

His arms tightened around her as if he were drawing

strength from her. "I've been thinking about Joanne a lot lately, and I only met her once; I hardly knew her," Jennifer said.

"She has been on my mind too, especially since we started on this trip, and because of Chris, I guess."

A great weariness spread over Jennifer. She was tired from the riding and hiking they had done that day, and now she was drained emotionally as well.

The wind had lost its force and become a gentle sighing in the trees. Jennifer picked up their mugs and saw that they still held some rum. "Here, let's finish these." They drank in silence. While Jennifer put the mugs in the little sink, Brian filled the stove for the night with as much wood as it could hold.

"I hope it stops snowing so we can find where Sam goes," she said, and meant it more than she could ever have imagined she could.

As she started climbing into the top bunk, Brian took her in his arms and pressed her close to him and kissed her.

"Goodnight," she said softly.

"Are you sure you want the top bunk?"

"Yes, it'll be warmer."

"All right, goodnight."

Sleep eluded Jennifer. The desire to have Brian hold her in his arms until she fell asleep had increased of late. And after the revealing talk they had just had, when she witnessed his suffering and guilt, she wished even more that there was room for two in the bunk so that she could lie with him and ease his pain and sorrow. Then she thought of Chris, and her face grew hot with shame as she recalled feelings of dislike towards him. She wished she could erase the evil thoughts and take back the angry words she had spoken on the trail. If she had only known, she kept thinking over and over. Now she understood some of the mystery that surrounded the two families. And her heart went out to all of them. She hoped the new baby would help them to overcome the sorrow of the past, and take some of the sting from remembering. She wondered if Brian would get over his guilt feeling about Joanne, and hoped and prayed he would, as now she knew it to be the obstacle that stood between them and their happiness; that, and Christopher's rejection of her, which must be resolved. She thought of how Joanne must have suffered in order to leave her beautiful little son and a husband as wonderful as Brian. She wept silently, until total exhaustion overcame her and she fell into a deep sleep.

Brian wasn't able to go to sleep either when he got into his sleeping bag even with the help of the rum. A million thoughts were going through his mind. If they didn't find Sam, Chris would blame Jennifer. Poor Jennifer, he hadn't been fair to her from the start, and now he felt guilty about that too.

The compassion and understanding she had shown him earlier was what had attracted him to her in the first place. But it wasn't working out for Chris, God damn it. Maybe Chris hadn't been ready.

And then he gave way to the thoughts of Joanne that were crowding his mind. He had failed her too. What a rotten son of a bitch he had been to her. Losing his patience with her illness when all the time she couldn't help it, but he hadn't known that then. He had tried to make her stand up and live as if she wasn't sick. For Chris, he said, everything was for Chris, but he couldn't help it. His son was an extension of himself, and he wanted everything to be perfect for him. But, shit, he couldn't even understand his son anymore. He was just a God damn failure, that's all he was. He didn't have the guts of his father and grandfather. He just couldn't seem to do a bloody thing right.

The rum was having its effect on Brian. He looked up and saw the reflection of the fire on the ceiling of the little cabin, and it started moving around in his head like a kaleidoscope. First he was in a church with candles and ladies in red dresses. Then there was a clear picture of Joanne walking down the aisle on her father's arm, smiling, beautiful. Pictures of snow and the exaltation of skiing. Joanne's laughter coming to him as she passed him on the slopes. The lodge at Lake Louise. More flashes of the joy and happiness that spanned ten wonderful years. There were flashes of a baby and a sheep. Then a clear picture of Joanne saying, "Sam's coming here has a meaning."

"What meaning?" he asked.

"I don't know, but we will find out eventually."

He had a flash of Joanne smiling when she handed baby Christopher to him. Brian turned over in his bunk and groaned in misery. How could he have failed someone so sweet and wonderful. He wished he could puke his guts out.

The rum finally had its effect on Brian and he fell into a stupor, while outside the wind died and the air turned warm. The snow started melting on the roof and dripped to the ground.

And the Otterhead River rose and flowed past the wardens' station in a torrent, as the melting snow engorged it almost to the brink of its banks.

13   A Battle

When the snowstorm started and the riders were no longer able to see ahead, Sam changed his course. He had left the side of the Otterhead River when he had come to a small creek feeding it from the steep side of its banks, and gone over into the next ravine where he had encountered a herd of his own kind, with a big old ram as ruler.

He had a subordinate, a smaller ram whom he dominated because of his size, who went along with everything the old ram did. He guarded the ewes and helped himself to them, while the old ram fought to retain his right to them, but what purpose he served other than a side kick was hard to tell. He followed the old ram wherever he went. And after the rutting season he followed him back to the male gang.

Rams band together after the mating season and stay together until the next fall. While the ewes do the same thing. The oldest ewe in the herd rules over the females and guides them through the lambing in the spring and the summer until the fall when rutting season comes, and the rams return to fight over the ewes for their right to claim them.

When Sam found the herd of sheep in the ravine with the old ram in charge, he moved boldly towards him and gestured at him by raising his leg and swinging it toward the other ram without striking him. The old ram wasn't accepting the insult, so he moved back about twenty paces and the fight was on. Both rams made a few quick steps towards each other, reared up with their front legs hanging straight and their necks bowed. And then when they were only a few feet apart, hurled themselves at each other and met in mid air with a jarring crash, horn to horn, the crash ringing out through the wind and falling snow. The impact was so fierce their bodies whiplashed, and they stood with their tails standing up so dazed with shock they stood staring off into space. Then they turned, and starting from the same position repeated the charge. Sam stopped to jam the ends of his horns into the ground and paw the earth and snow like an angry bull, but the act did not deter his opponent.

They fought on and on into the night while the wind blew and the snow piled up on the ground around them. And finally, when both rams began to tire, the fighting became more sinister. Sam narrowly missed a flying hoof, while Sam's hoof unintentionally came within inches of the old ram's testicles.

The subordinate ram came to see how the contest was progressing. He looked for a minute as if he would join in and then seemed to change his mind, as the old ram was nearly done. Finally the old ram broke off the engagement, and headed off down the mountain with his side kick in tow. Sam followed them a short way to make sure they were leaving for good, then he returned to claim his prize. One of the females was already in heat, and Sam fell in love with her right away and proceeded to plant his seed.

1·4   Search for Answers

The occupants of the wardens' cabin on the Otterhead River woke in the morning to a cloudless sky and a gentle breeze. The snow was almost gone. The river had crested in the pre-dawn hours and receded to almost the size it was the night before. Brian and Chris emerged from the cabin with their fishing poles in hand to try their luck in the eddies of the stream. Silver was instantly at their side for his morning greeting and a pat on the head.

Brian helped Chris untangle his line and choose the right fly, then he cast in and watched the water carry his line into a silent pool by some rocks where a log lay, half submerged. He was just starting to get that good feeling that comes to a fisherman anticipating the pleasure of landing a big trout when Chris, who had sidled over beside him, asked, "Do you think Jennifer will wait here while we go to find Sam?"

"Why?"

"Because I don't want her to come with us." Chris had decided to make a last bold attempt at leaving Jennifer behind.

Brian's anticipated pleasure in landing a sprightly trout faded as concern over his son's words took its place.

"But she won't hold us up any more; she can ride and handle her horse just fine," Brian said, hoping to change Christopher's mind.

"That's not why I don't want her," Chris said evasively.

"Why don't you want her then? What have you got against her anyway?"

Brian was exasperated again, trying to imagine his son's reason for not wanting Jennifer along.

"I don't want her to be with us when Sam gets there, that's all," Chris said petulantly.

As Brian looked at the tears gathering in the corners of his son's eyes while his face tightened in determination, he suspected that there was a more serious reason behind Chris wanting to follow Sam than just to find out where he went. Trying to imagine what other reasons Chris may have filled him with dread. What had started out to be a ride in the hills with his son on a long weekend in Indian Summer to see where the sheep went, had become more and more complicated, and the complications started when Jennifer announced that she wanted to come along. His heart beat heavily in his chest as he pondered a way to get Chris to tell him why he had turned against Jennifer when he had liked her at first and even called her Mom, when Chris spoke again.

"Jennifer doesn't like Sam."

"Sure she does." He could see that he hadn't convinced Chris, so he said, "Remember yesterday when she saw Sam in the meadow. She said that he was beautiful and that there was something mysterious about him. She wouldn't have said those things if she didn't love him."

"But before that she said he was a stupid sheep, and Mommy never said bad things about Sam even when he wasted the hay and chased the horses. Mommy loves Sam and he's hers, isn't he, he belongs to her."

"She loved him all right, but I think she felt that he belonged to you, seeing as he came the day you were born," Brian said.

"She must love him lots or she wouldn't have taken all those pictures of him, would she? They're friends," Chris said emphatically.

"I guess you're right; she did love him lots, and they were

friends." There was sadness in Brian's voice as he thought of the love and understanding Joanne had for Sam.

"And she wants us to look after him too, doesn't she?"

"Yes, she would want us to look after him. Is that why we're following him, to look after him for Mommy?"

"It's what she wants and it's what I want too, to go where Sam goes."

"Okay, we're going." Children are so simple, Brian thought; it's adults that complicate things. All Chris wanted to do was protect Sam because of his mother, and his reason for not wanting Jennifer along probably had something to do with his loyalty, and was best left alone. Chris would understand in time.

Brian's thoughts were interrupted by a tug on his line and the reel of his rod hummed the tune every fisherman longs to hear.

Chris watched as Brian skilfully landed a beautiful rainbow trout, while Sam bounded along the bank participating in the excitement.

"Trout for breakfast, Chris. Come on, there's fish in there, cast in," Brian said, hoping to divert Chris from the trauma that was bringing tears to his eyes. Brian and Chris spent the ensuing hour casting, landing, and then cleaning a catch of trout to ensure a hearty breakfast for them all.

Tom poured coffee for himself and Jennifer as soon as she was up, and the two of them sat down at the table to enjoy their first savory cup of the day. They could see Brian and Chris down by the river and knew there would be fish for breakfast.

"Chris must have had a bad nightmare last night," Tom remarked. "He even woke me up."

"Oh, why," Jennifer said in surprise as she hadn't been aware that Chris was subject to nightmares and it disturbed her.

"I haven't known him to have one before."

"Well, he sure must have had one last night. He was sobbing in his sleep, and I thought I heard him trying to say 'Mommy.' Maybe I should have awakened you when he was trying to call you, but I was pretty groggy from the effects of the rum."

Jennifer stared at Tom, alarmed by what he had told her. "He calls me Jennifer now," she blurted before realizing that Tom didn't know she wasn't Christopher's real mother. "I'm his stepmother. And I hate that name; it reminds me of all the wicked stepmothers in children's fairy tales."

Tom could see that he had upset Jennifer by telling her about Christopher's nightmare, and wished he had kept his mouth shut, because he remembered hearing Chris call her by her first name and had been surprised at the time. Before he could offer his apologies, she spoke again.

"Christopher's real mother died, and he called her Mommy." Tom remembered the deep love he saw in Jennifer's eyes when she looked at Brian and realized the reason she had ventured along on a trip that she was totally unprepared for was to be close to him. But now as he sat watching her he suspected there was a problem between the three of them, and wondered if Jennifer and Chris were competing for Brian's attention.

"It's more difficult than I imagined being a second wife." There was something about this friendly man that made Jennifer feel she could confide in him.

"I'm sure it is, how long have you been married?"

"Not very long, four and a half months," she said.

"Well, it takes time to adjust to marriage, even a first marriage, and a second marriage is bound to have more problems. In your case there's three of you to adjust. But when people love each other things work out in time." Tom wanted to remove the worried look from her pretty face and see her smile again.

"That's the problem. Chris isn't accepting me because he doesn't love me."

"Sure he loves you, they both do." It was so obvious to Tom, by the way they looked at her, and yet this woman sat there eating her heart out, doubting it. For a minute he was glad that he wasn't young any more. "He's just not used to sharing his father, that's all, but he will, just give him time."

"I hope you're right, Tom," she said with new hope, her spirits rising.

"I'm right, you just wait and see, and be patient. He's just

"I'm right, you just wait and see, and be patient. He's just confused about where his loyalties lie, that's all, that's why he was calling for his mother in his sleep."

"I think you're right. I hope you are. Oh, Tom, you've really helped me, thank you so much." All three of us are confused, she thought. She knew about Brian, but she hadn't thought of Chris feeling guilty. That would explain a lot of things, but wondered what it had to do with following Sam. She knew that they must find Sam.

Chris burst into the cabin displaying their catch of fish with pride. Tom had the frying pans already heating on the stove, so they hosted up a breakfast of trout and toast fit for a king. They sat around sipping coffee while the fish bones dried on their plates. Chris wiped the crumbs from his mouth with the back of his hand. He knew from other trips into the mountains with his father that you could get away with a lot of things out in the wilds that you couldn't at home. The men forgot their manners some, and although Jennifer was along this time, even she didn't seem to notice things as much. He rested his head in his hands with his elbows on the table and waited for a lull in the conversation so he could say what was on his mind. "How soon are we going to start looking for Sam?"

"As soon as we're ready," Brian said. Chris was watching him intently, and Brian suspected that Chris was waiting for him to ask Jennifer to stay behind, which he had no intention of doing. It pleased him to see that she looked rested and seemed to be in good spirits as she laughed and joked with Tom, and he hoped Chris would not start showing his reluctance to have her along.

"If you are planning on going up to that area where I saw the ewes, you may as well just take what you need for the day and leave the rest of your gear here, and plan on spending tonight with me. There is no way you can go up there and back and then start for home. It's just too far," Tom said.

"If you wouldn't mind putting up with us again, Tom, that would be great, thanks," Brian said. When he saw Jennifer's grateful smile he added, "I think Jennifer finds it a little more comfortable than a tent." It was a relief to him having her understand his need to find the ram for Chris instead of wanting to return home as she had done previously. "My hope is that we can find him around here, and we won't have to go that far."

"Even if you do pick up his trail around here, where he's headed is where those ewes are, I'd bet on that; so if you're going to follow him, you will still have to go up there. As a matter of fact, I doubt if he even crossed the river when we did, no reason for him to."

"Is there no way we could go back to where we crossed and pick up his trail from there?" Brian asked.

"To travel with horses on the other side of the Otterhead at this point is impossible."

"Well, we'd better get started then," Brian said, getting up from the table. He saw that Chris was watching Jennifer intently as if he were looking for an opportunity to speak, and fearing what he was about to say, said "Chris, how about you giving me a hand saddling the horses?"

"Okay," Chris said reluctantly, as he was about to suggest to Jennifer that she could stay at the cabin if she liked as they would be back tonight, but he knew by the tone of his father's voice that he wasn't giving him a choice about helping with the saddling; so he slid off his chair and headed for the door, hoping to speak to Jennifer later.

Tom followed Brian and Chris out to the horses and showed them where they could picket the pack horse to graze for the day, as there was no need for her to be taken along.

Brian had enjoyed his evening's conversation with Tom and felt he wouldn't mind having him join them for the day's ride. "What are your plans for the day, Tom? Any chance of your coming with us?"

"Thanks, but I'd better get looking for whoever it is doing the hunting in this area, and I gotta get on the radio phone to that Game Warden friend of yours in Golden, to get him watching in his area. Want me to send a message home for you?"

"That would be great if you would; ask him to call my father, Russell Logan, and tell him we are fine and that we'll be a day late getting home."

"Okay, I'll do that."

"Thanks, Tom, that chance meeting with you has worked out real good for us," Brian said, pleased.

When they had the horses watered and saddled, Brian went back to the cabin to tell Jennifer they were ready to leave.

"I sure hope you find where that sheep of yours goes, young fellow," Tom said as he and Chris stood with the horses waiting for Brian and Jennifer.

"He's going to heaven; that's where he's going. Is that where you saw those other sheep, in heaven?" Chris asked.

Tom threw back his head and roared with laughter. "I guess you could call it heaven. That ram of yours will think so, anyway, if he wins his right to the females."

Chris was happy when he learned that Tom thought where Sam went was heaven, and his father would know how to go there. He didn't mind Jennifer coming along now that she had learned how to ride, but he was trying to think what to do about her when they got there. Then he remembered Tom saying it was steep and rocky and that they would have to leave the horses and do some climbing; so there would be no problem. She would have to stay with the horses as she didn't know how to climb up rock cliffs anyway. When Brian and Jennifer arrived, they were surprised to find Chris in a good mood as they both expected him to object to Jennifer coming along.

They said goodbye to Tom and rode away along the hiking trail just as the sun's rays slanted down into the valley where the Otterhead River flows. They searched along the banks in the soft earth and patches of remaining snow for Sam's tracks, and after finding no trace they turned and rode up the river in the direction of the valley where Tom had seen the sheep earlier. The wind had stripped the trees of their remaining leaves, leaving the branches stark against the autumn sky, suggesting a more sinister season, and the hiking trail was strewn with branches.

As the riders progressed up the valley, the river grew gradually smaller, and the mountain, which was steep and rocky across from the warden's station, looked more accessible. They came to a glade where the river flowed over a gravel bed. It was shallow, so they crossed it with ease, and rode along the bank on the other side. When they came to the end of the steep mountain, they were able to ride over a smaller one beside it and travel in the valley on the other side. Again they rode with Brian in the lead, Chris in the middle and Jennifer in the rear, while Silver scouted the flanks. When the valley narrowed with rocky cliffs on either side, they reined in and agreed that it looked like the place Tom had described having seen the sheep.

It was obvious that Silver, who had been sniffing around, had found some tracks as he became very excited. This confirmed the riders' belief that they were in the right place and Sam had passed that way.

"I'll climb up the cliff and see what's on the other side, while you two wait here. No use all of us climbing a cliff like that for nothing," Brian said.

"I want to go with you, Dad," Chris said.

"I think you should stay with Jennifer."

"I stayed the other times, so can I go this time, please?"

"I don't mind staying by myself if you want to take him." Jennifer looked at the rocky cliffs that surrounded the glade and thought it a pretty safe place to wait. There wasn't likely to be any danger from slides or animals charging out of the bush. There was no bush and the rock cliffs looked very solid.

"We won't be long," Brian said as they all dismounted.

"I'll just sit on those rocks and soak up some sun. You don't have to hurry," Jennifer said, approaching some rocks that were flat on top. She could lie down if she wanted to. She sat down and watched Brian and Chris climb the cliff with interest. The man and the boy picked their way up the face of the cliff without much difficulty. When they reached the top, Brian waved to Jennifer and then they disappeared out of sight.

Jennifer leaned back and let the warm sun shine on her face. Indian summer wasn't over, after all, and water from the melting snow was trickling down the rocks on the face òf the cliff. She was pleased that the weather promised a few more days of Indian summer, which was a bonus as they had already enjoyed ten beautiful days. She wasn't in a hurry for winter if it was anything like the misery she had suffered in the freak storm the day before.

She watched the horses graze on the dry grass and heard some birds chirping off somewhere. Awareness of the tranquility that was in the little glen awoke in Jennifer, and she breathed in the pure fresh air, and looked at her surroundings with new eyes. And a peace she had never known before entered her soul. This then is what people seek, she thought, this awareness of nature that replenishes, the rest from care, and she was glad that she had found it. After her talk with Brian the night before about Joanne, she felt a deep sadness for the girl who no longer shared these wonderful experiences with her husband and son.

She glanced up to the top of the cliff and saw Brian standing there beckoning her. They must have found something, she thought, and hoped with all her heart that they had found Sam. She got up and started to climb the cliff without giving any thought to the difficulty of the task. After being in the wild country for two days and watching Brian and Chris climb she had learned a few things, and the knack of ascending the cliff seemed to come to her as she climbed, and she reached the top with a feeling of accomplishment. She took a breath of the fragrant air and smiled at the look of pride on Brian's face.

Brian was surprised and pleased at the way Jennifer had manipulated her way up the difficult face of the cliff. He reached out and took her in his arms and gave her a kiss, then said, "There are some sheep across the ravine on top of a ridge, and we think the ram in charge must be Sam or we couldn't have got so close."

"Oh, I hope it's Sam! It must be, don't you think?" Jennifer said with excitement. Brian took Jennifer's hand and led her through a shelter of pines, and then he signaled to her to get down on her hands and knees like him, and they crawled through the tall dry grass to the edge of a ravine where Chris and Silver lay hidden by shrubs watching the sheep on a ridge across the ravine. Chris turned to look at them as they crawled up beside him, but the look he gave Jennifer was not one of welcome. He's up to something, she thought, and she wondered what it could be; he was scheming, she was sure of that. She looked across the ravine at the sheep and prayed that the ram was Sam.

Brian took the binoculars from Chris and studied the sheep and then put them down and turned to Chris with a big smile. "It's Sam all right, I can see that tuft of hair on the back of his head."

"I knew it, I knew it was Sam!" Chris was so pleased and excited he could hardly contain himself.

"Shhh, Sam knows us but the others don't, and sheep have a keen sense of hearing," Brian told Chris.

"Sam's the boss though, isn't he?"

"It looks like he's got himself a harem all right; yes, I guess he's the boss. He's been in a fight, too. He looks a little beaten up. He must have been; those ewes he's with weren't alone. There was a ram there, and Sam fought him and won."

"Good for Sam," Jennifer said. "I'm proud of him." She wondered what all the fuss with Chris was about, as he seemed to be contented watching the sheep. Then she remembered the scheming look she saw on Chris' face when she and Brian crawled up beside him. Chris had some other plans, she was sure of it. She watched the two of them lying beside her watching the sheep. She felt excluded but did not feel sorry for herself.

"I think Sam came up here yesterday when we crossed the river with Tom and went to his cabin. Sam probably arrived in the evening and fought the ram that was here. Which means he has found his mates and there will be some little Sams running around next spring," Brian said.

"Can we come and see them?" Chris asked.

"We probably will. What do you think, Jennifer?" Brian asked.

"I think it would be fun; yes, I'd love to," and knew she meant it. She thought of how beautiful it would be here in the spring. She recalled Tom saying that the sheep come down at this time of year for food when snow falls on the upper levels. To see the lambs meant going higher up into the mountains and found that she would be looking forward to it through the winter. She wondered how long a pregnant woman could ride a

169

horse, and was disappointed to think she may have to stay at home. She had experienced a bit of nausea that morning when the fish were frying, which she had managed to conceal from the men, but it was returning as she lay on her stomach watching the sheep. She decided to leave them alone for a while.

"I think I'll go back to the cliff and check on the horses," she said.

Chris looked pleased as she made a motion to crawl back to the pines, but Brian looked at her in alarm, as he noticed the whiteness of her face.

"Are you all right?" he asked with concern.

"I'm fine, I just need to walk around a bit, that's all."

She reached the pines and stood up, relieved. She took several deep breaths of the pine-scented air and felt her nausea subside with relief. She reached the edge of the cliff and looked down at the horses, who gave her an unconcerned look and continued grazing. She sat on a log where she could see up a draw between the mountains, and the view was breath-taking. There were several rugged peaks jutting into the sky, and the effect of the sun glistening on the snow gave the illusion of jewels that could be touched by reaching out a hand. The way distances could look so close and be so far away in the mountains surprised Jennifer. She sat gazing at the peaks that seemed to reach into the very heavens, entranced. She laughed at herself when she realized how much she had come to love "Brian's hills." There was something about the beauty of nature that got to a person, she thought, like finding your roots, earth to earth, something like that.

After Jennifer left, Brian and Chris lay watching Sam with his mate, discussing the lambs that would be born in the spring. Silver lay beside them dozing in the noonday sun. They talked quietly, not wanting to chance disturbing the sheep across the ravine. They were quiet for a time, and then Chris slid over closer to Brian.

"Is this heaven, Dad?"

"For Sam it is, I guess; he looks pretty happy and proud, don't you think?" Brian said, amused.

"If this is really heaven, then where is Mommy? Because I want to ask her to come home."

Brian turned and looked at his son in utter astonishment. He had been trying to get to the bottom of his son's reason for following Sam by discussing the lambs and the life of the sheep. But the question Chris asked shook him badly. Before he could think of an answer, Chris spoke again.

"You said Mommy has gone to heaven; so where is she?" Chris asked in a demanding voice.

"Not this kind of heaven, Chris."

"What then?"

"God's heaven."

"Where is God's heaven?"

"Nobody really knows."

"It's in the sky. Kevin's mother said it's in the sky, and the mountains touch the sky. Sam knows where Mommy is. He goes there; I want to find Mommy and ask her to come back. Kevin's mother went away when she had a fight with his Dad but she came back. Did you and Mommy have a fight?" Chris was very worked up and the words came tumbling out.

"No, Chris, your mother was sick and she lost the fight with life." Brian as filled with remorse for letting Chris think he could ask his mother to come back; he really had bungled things.

"No, I'm going to find her. Sam goes to her, I know he does. We have to follow him again when he leaves here, if this isn't heaven." Chris was beside himself.

Brian groped for a way to calm Chris down so he could explain to him, as there was no way of making him understand in the state he was in. He glanced across the ravine and saw a strange ram emerge from the bush. "There's another ram over there now." He pointed across the ravine. Jennifer crawled up beside Brian and saw him pointing as the strange ram approached Sam, and watched, fascinated. She noticed the look of wretchedness on Brian's face and one of determination on Christopher's, and thought that something had transpired between the two of them in her absence.

"What's happening over there?" she asked.

171

"Sam is being challenged," Brian said, as the strange ram went up to Sam and bumped him with his shoulder.

"Sam is being challenged and he is going to have to fight the new ram, to retain his right to the ewes. It looks like they are about the same size and have the same size horns, so it should be an even fight," Brian said.

"I hope Sam wins," Chris said, frightened.

"He will, Chris; we'll all pull for him so he has to," Jennifer said.

The fight that followed was even. The two animals hurled themselves at each other and met in mid air with a clash of horns that resounded through the mountains. Again and again they hurled themselves at each other and rebounded, stunned. It went on and on, neither seeming to gain ground until the watchers noticed that on each rebound Sam, whose back was to the edge of the cliff, was coming closer and closer to the edge. They stood up and yelled at the top of their lungs, trying to stop the fight, but it was too late. On the next clash Sam lost his footing and hurtled down over the precipice onto the jagged rocks below, to the horror of the three Logans who stood watching.

"Sam! Sam!" Chris yelled as they all three started down the bank to the floor of the ravine, where Sam lay still upon the rocks where he had fallen. The strange ram and the ewes bounded off into the bush across the ravine, their rumps bouncing up and down like white pillows in the afternoon sun. Brian reached Sam first and felt for his heart beat, but there was none. His heart sank at this dreadful happening that he must explain to Chris.

Chris was crying when he and Jennifer reached the place where Sam lay, and stood waiting for Brian to tell him of Sam's condition.

Brian kept running his hands over the ram's body trying to think of a way to break the terrible news to Chris, but words escaped him. When the air became strained with expectancy, he could delay no longer. He stood up and said, "Sam broke his neck when he fell so he didn't suffer. I'm sorry Chris, but Sam is dead."

"No, no, no, he can't be, he can't be," Chris sobbed hysterically. Jennifer was fighting her own tears but managed to say, "But he is, dear."

"Now I'll never find Mommy," Chris sobbed as he was seized with that same terror he had felt on that awful day when his mother had driven away.

"Find your mother?" Jennifer looked at Brian incredulously. "What does he mean?"

"Sam was going to take me to Mommy and I was going to ask her to come back," Chris blurted between sobs. "I want her to come back. I miss her."

"No, Chris," was all Jennifer could say through her tears, while Brian stood helplessly by, clenching and unclenching his fists, shocked by his son's revelation.

"Yes, yes, yes," Chris wailed while wiping tears away with the backs of both hands.

Brian came to where Chris and Jennifer stood and tried to put his arms around his son, but Chris pulled away and cried harder than ever. Brian looked at Jennifer helplessly. She saw the look of suffering in his eyes and took a step towards him to comfort him, but he turned and walked away.

"I'll find a spot to bury Sam," he said in a choked voice. Christopher went and laid his head on Sam's neck and sobbed uncontrollably while Jennifer tried in vain to console him.

Brian found a spot in the bottom of the ravine where the earth was soft with leaves and moss. He scooped out a grave for Sam as best he could with a piece of wood.

Jennifer helped Brian drag Sam's body to the grave, and Chris followed, sobbing all the way. They laid Sam in the shallow grave, and Brian started covering him with what little earth he had been able to remove.

Christopher's crying turned to near hysteria when he saw the body of his beloved Sam disappearing under the cover of earth. "Come back Sam, come back, I need you, I need you to find Mommy." He wanted to run and hold onto Sam so that his father couldn't cover him with earth, but the pain in his chest was so intense that he couldn't move.

173

"He can't come back, Chris." Brian said with sobs in his voice.

"Can't Mommy come back either?"

"No, she can't come back either, Chris." It was the hardest thing Brian had ever had to do, but he knew it must be done.

"Is my mother in the ground too? Is she, Dad?"

"Her spirit is in heaven, just her body is in the ground the same as Sam's." Jennifer was filled with compassion for the suffering that Chris was enduring, as she tried to take him in her arms, but he pushed her away.

"I love you, Chris, don't you know that? I know how hard this is for you and I want to help you," Jennifer pleaded.

"Jennifer, I was going to tell Mommy I'm sorry for being bad and ask her to forgive me and to come home," Chris sobbed harder. "That's why she went away, because I was bad."

"No, darling, you were not bad and your mother loved you very much. She went because she was too sick to stay here, that's all." She reached out for him again, as a strong desire to comfort him filled her.

He took a step towards her and seemed to crumple into her arms. She held him close against her breast and let him vent his pent-up sorrow.

Brian continued filling the grave. He stopped to wipe the corners of his eyes with the backs of his hands while he had trouble swallowing. He was shovelling the dirt over Sam's body so fast he ran out of breath. He couldn't stand the sound of his son's sobs. I made a mistake, he thought. All this heartbreak because I was too big a coward to tell Chris the truth about Joanne's death. To say she had gone to heaven was the easy way out at the time, and then somehow Chris got the idea that she could come back, because his friend's mother came back. He should have made him understand that it was final, that she was gone and couldn't come back. Brian's own distress increased, when he realized that he too had kept the feeling that she would return. He himself had not accepted the finality of death. And the ram whom Joanne had loved so much kept the feeling alive.

Brian looked at his son crying his heart out, for his lost

sheep and for his chance to see his mother, and he knew that he must help him to understand. He couldn't fail him again.

He prayed for words of comfort for Chris, without having to reveal the true nature of his mother's illness, that had resulted in her death. Someday he was going to have to make Chris understand how his mother had suffered, how they had all suffered as a result of that sad, cruel illness that sometimes inflicts its merciless domain over the minds of man. Its elusive mystery secreting its power over its victims since the beginning of time, and still eluding medical science. That deceptive monster that lurks in the mind, allows its victims periods of normalcy, then plunges them down into the depths of depression, for no known reason, a merry-go-round of torment that ends in madness or death. The cruelty of it was like a knife in Brian's heart.

"Chris," he said, "you must understand that life is hard, and sometimes seems to us to be cruel, but there is a reason for everything, although we may not understand so at the time. But death is a part of life. It is the way of things. Life isn't forever, not for anything, everything has a beginning and end."

"No," Chris cried. "No." The tightness in his chest was getting worse, and he could hardly breathe.

"Yes, Chris, you must learn to accept things as they are, the way life is, we can't change that."

As Chris cried harder, Brian looked down at the dead grass at his feet and at the falling yellow leaves, while he struggled to control his own emotions. Then he said, "Look at the dead grass, Chris, it only lived for one season, but new grass will come in the spring, and the leaves that have withered and died. They are falling to the ground in acceptance of change, and are becoming part of the earth, and in the spring new leaves will grow. Sam was getting old, and he didn't have many years left. He accepted the challenge of life, and he also accepted death. He knew that life goes on and that the dead live on in their descendants, and in the minds of the living."

Chris was watching Brian, and his tears had subsided, but spilled down his cheeks again as he spoke, "But Mommy wasn't old." A picture of her beautiful face came into his mind and smote his heart.

"No, but she was very sick, and life isn't good when you're sick. She accepted death as an end to her suffering."

"Why, why was she sick?" And why, he wondered, hadn't he known she was sick when she left.

"I don't know, Chris, that's one of the things we have to accept that we can't change."

Brian looked at his son and knew it wasn't enough. Then something Joanne had written in her journal in acceptance of her illness, after an endless round of doctors, diets, and medication, her great achievements on her highs and the hell of the lows, came to him.

"It was her karma," he said sadly.

Chris was watching him as if he were trying to comprehend what Brian had said, and then he asked, "Was this Sam's karma too, do you think?"

"It must have been, Mommy would have thought it was."

"Well I don't like it." Chris said as his jaw tightened and his fists came up to wipe the tears from his cheeks.

Brian went to his son and took him in his arms, and as Chris leaned against him, he tightened his arms around him and kissed him. "I love you, Chris," he said.

"I love you too, Dad," Chris said in a choked voice. "But I wish it didn't have to be that way with Mommy, and Sam."

"I wish so too," Brian said. "Mommy loved you very much, and it wasn't because of you that she died. You must never think that. You were always a good boy, and Mommy thought you were wonderful. You made her proud and happy that you were ours."

"It was because of her karma then, wasn't it, that she got sick and everything? Does karma mean when it's your turn?" Chris asked.

"Something like that," Brian said, wishing he could convince himself that was why it was, but he still had doubts about his own part in it all, his own inadequacy, his failure to understand and help her.

"Well, it sure makes people sad and unhappy when it's your

karma," Chris said with a bit of a sob. He knew now that it wasn't because of him that his mother had gone away, but the sight of her car disappearing in the dust, and the feeling that he had of wanting to run after her, would be with him forever.

Then Brian put his arms around Jennifer as well, and she could no longer hold back the sorrow that filled her and she cried harder as she had come to love that beautiful proud wild ram. She felt that Chris and Brian were not only losing Sam but Joanne as well, as they had both been hanging on to her through the ram somehow.

Not knowing what it must be like to lose someone you dearly love, she had been insensitive to their needs, and she wanted to tell them so. As a thought came to her she said, "The greatest cruelty of man to man is failing to understand. Even people who love each other don't understand each other's needs; that's why we are alone. Maybe we are so involved with our own needs we are insensitive to the needs of others."

"Like us, Jennifer?" Brian asked.

"Yes, like us. Like all three of us," and she tightened her arm around Christopher, and he nodded his head in agreement.

"I think you just said something very meaningful, but look at how hard we tried. I think we have found each other's needs, or some of them, anyway. Why don't we keep on trying?" Brian said, as he kissed the top of Christopher's curly head, and prayed that he would never again fail to meet the needs of his son.

"Sounds like a good idea to me," she said.

They stood in the wilderness in the Indian summer sun, a man, a woman, and a child with arms entwined, not speaking, the closeness being more intense that way. Strength to bear their own burden increased as they embraced each other's sorrow. And the plague of anger and resentment that accompany misunderstanding drifted away and they became one. One family unit of love. And so they stood giving and receiving and sharing, until Brian spoke.

"We'd better put rocks on Sam's grave to protect it."

So they gathered rocks and piled them on Sam's grave.

They piled the stones much higher than was needed for protection. They were paying a last tribute to Sam.

"We need something for a marker," Jennifer said. Brian cut cedar boughs which Chris and Jennifer wound into a wreath while Brian tied two sticks together for a cross, and anchored it in the rocks at Sam's head. Chris hung the wreath on the cross, and Jennifer said a little prayer when Chris asked her to.

"Now we will be able to find it again when we come to see the baby lambs in the spring. Do you think Sam's really going to have some babies?" Christopher's child's mind was already looking to something else, something ahead, something that makes life continue.

"Pretty sure, Chris. That would be nice, wouldn't it, some more little Sams running around up here," Brian said.

"But where are they now?"

Brian looked at Jennifer as if to say this is where you take over. So she went to Chris and said, "The ewes have the babies in their stomachs."

"But how does it work?" Chris asked with interest.

"Nature took a little tiny piece from every piece of Sam's body and put it into a sperm, and Sam put his sperm into the ewe's body and it joined her egg. The lamb will grow from the egg, and the genes will determine what the lamb will be. It could be a ram, and look just like Sam with big horns and bright eyes; it could inherit Sam's wisdom and courage too. The lamb will grow inside the ewe until it's big enough to be born in the spring." Jennifer saw that Chris was listening intently, and looked pleased.

"When we come in the spring, we will be able to see which is Sam's because it will look like him," Chris said in awe.

"It could; wouldn't that be wonderful." She was glad to see that Chris was feeling better with the thought of the lambs.

"It would kinda be like having Sam, wouldn't it? When the lamb grows up, maybe it will even come to live at Windsong," Chris said.

"Maybe. Anyway, Sam will live on through his offspring, and that's a nice thought," she said.

"I think we're going to have to be on our way pretty soon if we want to get back to Tom's cabin by dark," Brian said.

"We'll be back, Sam," Chris said as he lay his hand on the mound of rocks in a last loving gesture.

They made their way up the side of the ravine and reached the spot where they had watched the rams fight earlier. They turned and stood silently looking with sadness down at the mound of rocks on the ravine floor with the cross and wreath of cedar boughs. Then they walked through the grove of pines and climbed down the steep face of the cliff to the waiting horses. The rays of the sun were suggesting late afternoon as they mounted and rode in the direction they had come. They crossed the river at the same shallow gravel bed where they had crossed in the morning and found the hiking trail that would take them to the wardens' station. The sky was clear and the sun shone, but there was a coolness in the air that meant the warm days of Indian summer were drawing to a close.

The river beside the trail had a melody more in keeping with the size of its banks. The runoff from the melting snow had subsided. The wind had swept the leaves into drifts along the sides of the path, and the deep shade of the forest was green with velvet moss. The snowberry bushes at the side of the trail had a bumper crop. The leaves had dropped, but the white waxy berries were clustered to the tops of the branches, which meant a winter with lots of snow, Brian explained. It was nature's way of seeing that the birds had food.

The sun had left the valley where the hiking trail wound its way along the river, so the riders traveled in cool shade. They stopped on top of a ridge to don their jackets before descending into the heavy timber where the shadows of evening were beginning to fall.

"There's some pink snow over there," Brian said, pointing to some rugged mountains in the distance where the last rays of the sun were kissing the peaks with a rosy hue.

Chris said, "Dad," in a voice that implied you can't fool me.

Jennifer enjoyed the beauty of the sight, then sighed for the ending day. The wrenching emotions she had been through had taken their toll and she was weary.

"There's some smoke in those trees down there; look. Is it a fire? Maybe it's a forest fire." Chris was pointing to some smoke that could be seen drifting skyward from the forest in the valley by the river.

"It looks more like a fire in Tom Shannon's stove to me," Brian said, pleased that their journey was coming to an end.

They all instinctively spurred their horses to hasten to the fire from which the smoke was ascending.

Tom heard Silver bark as they rode up to the cabin, so he opened the door to greet them. The looks on their faces told him that things had not gone well that day for them. He was about to greet them with a hearty welcome, thinking they would be happy after finding where the sheep went, but changed to a cheerful hello after seeing their anguished looks. Jennifer's response was the only one loud enough to hear. He saw Brian's lips move and that was all; so he grabbed his jacket from its hook beside the door and went to give Brian a hand unsaddling the horses.

"The cabin is nice and warm; you and Chris go inside," Tom said to Jennifer as she dismounted.

"Thanks, Tom," she said gratefully.

Christopher found it necessary to reveal what was on his mind. "Sam's dead, Tom; he got killed fighting. He would have won but he fell off the cliff." At that point he had to give up telling about Sam in order to stifle a sob.

Tom clearly understood the anguish which Chris was feeling, and spoke with sympathy.

"I'm sorry to hear that, Chris, really sorry," he said in a gentle voice.

The chill of night was descending with the evening shadows, and as Jennifer and Chris entered the cabin, they were greeted by warmth from a roaring fire. When Brian and Tom came in a few minutes later after leaving the horses to bed down for the night with Tom's horse, Chris and Jennifer were standing hugging the stove.

Tom spread his hands out over the heat and then rubbed them together as the kettle of water started to sing.

"Did I hear you say you have more rum, Brian?" he asked.

"Yes, I do." Brian went to his pack in the corner to get the extra bottle of rum he had brought along, just in case.

"Darned if I don't think what we all need here is a drink." Tom left the stove and went to the cupboard to prepare the mugs for the rum Brian was about to pour.

As Tom handed Jennifer a mug of hot spiced rum, he hoped a good stiff drink would help them all to relax as he was at a loss for what to say to cheer them up.

There was a large heavy pot sitting on the back of the stove, and a delicious aroma was escaping from under the lid where the handle of a spoon was protruding.

Tom saw Jennifer eye the pot with curiosity. "I hope you like stew." The look of relief on Jennifer's face, and a grin from Brian, convinced Tom that his efforts were not in vain. Chris looked uninterested and Tom understood him not wanting food after the ordeal he must have been through when his sheep died.

"Well, what are we all standing up for? Why don't we sit down, and you may as well take your jackets off," Tom said, pulling up a chair for Jennifer.

Tom had seen many beautiful wild animals lose their lives in his job, and it never stopped bothering him. He knew how a boy must feel losing an animal as majestic as a bighorn ram that had lived at his home all his life, and the parents must be feeling sorry for the boy. But he wished someone would say something to break the quiet. He could tell them about riding down and finding the wounded doe, that should get them out of their state of lethargy. He decided to tell them as much as he could about his day, and then relate an experience he had previously that might get Christopher's mind off his loss.

"I had an interesting day myself today."

"Yeah." Brian gave a minimum response, but Tom continued.

"First, it took an hour to get that radio phone working, as all they supply us with is junk the government can't use any place else. Anyhow, I finally got hold of your friend Farley in Golden and, by the way, he phoned your folks to say you would be late getting back home. He called me back later to say he had spoken to your father, Brian."

"Thanks, Tom," Brian said.

Tom continued, "Farley had lots of complaints this year about hunters. It seems some woman on a farm near Golden had a bullet whistle past her head when she was out in her own yard the other day. It's keeping him busy investigating all the local complaints; he said he would try to find time to check the area outside the park. But it's the weekend when all the first time hunting dudes from the city are out that things happen."

Tom leaned over and fed the fire from the pile of wood on the floor. He glanced around at the circle of faces and saw they were still overshadowed with gloom. Jennifer was listening to him, Brian half, but Chris not at all, but when he spoke again, he captured everyone's attention.

"Then I decided to ride down and see what became of the wounded doe I saw yesterday. I stopped by that campsite that didn't appeal to you people on the way up in the snow. And as it turns out, it's a good thing you didn't stay there as that is where the doe went for protection from the storm. All three Logans were listening eagerly for Tom to continue his story, and that pleased him.

"I found her in behind the chimney of the barbecue all snug, and you know, she is going to be just fine. I'll go back and check on her again tomorrow, but I'm sure she's going to make it." Chris had listened to every word, and some of the sorrow had gone from his face. Tom was encouraged, so he said, "How about if we try that stew and see if it's fit to eat, and I'll tell you about Mr. Pester."

"Mr. Pester, who's he?" Chris asked with something that resembled a smile on his face. He was so curious about Mr. Pester that he forgot to refuse the plate of stew Tom handed him because he wasn't hungry.

"Mr. Pester is a young cinnamon bear that pestered the campers at a campsite in the park last summer. He started by raiding their camps for food. He got so smart he could open an ice chest and feast on eggs, bacon, fried chicken, or any other goodies he could find, leaving the chest with only a few claw marks on it."

Chris was so amused by Mr. Pester that he forgot his troubles and ate some of his stew. And Tom could see a touch of laughter in his eyes.

"Well, that Mr. Pester got to be such a pest after he got used to finding his food so easily that we had to move him to another area and, you know, he found his way right back again. One day he even ate twenty five pounds of dog food, and drank a liter of motor boat oil as well."

They all laughed at that, and seemed to relax a little.

"Then what happened to him, Tom?" Chris asked.

"He got braver and braver. He started climbing on top of people's campers, so we had to pack him up and take him so far away into the wilds that he couldn't find his way back, and that's how we fixed Mr. Pester."

They ate the whole pot of stew along with a loaf of bread and butter. There wasn't anything left for Silver, so it was dog food for him that night.

When Jennifer saw that Chris was getting sleepy, she suggested bed and he went without any fuss.

Chris lay in his bunk thinking of his dream of the night before when he saw Sam running up the mountain to his mother. They are together now, he thought, so Mommy wouldn't be lonely. They are up there in the sky where the mountain peaks go, where else could heaven be. He was glad she hadn't left because he was bad. It made him feel a whole lot better knowing she left because she was sick.

"Dad, will you come here, please?"

Brian got up and went to the bunk to see what Chris wanted. When he saw the solemn look on Christopher's face he was reminded again of his grandfather Cyrus. That same strong self control that he had seen on Cyrus' face in times of sorrow he was now seeing in Chris, and he was proud of him.

"Dad, where is Mommy's grave?"

"In the cemetery in Golden beside my grandparents, Effie

and Cyrus. Do you know where the cemetery is?" Chris shook his head no.

"It's on the hill overlooking the valley, and it's very beautiful and peaceful there."

"Will you take me there? I want to see it."

"Yes, I'll take you there." Brian hadn't been there since that tragic time two years before, and he didn't want to go there now but he knew he must.

"Can we go when we get home?"

"Well, there will be school first and lots of things to get caught up on at Windsong, but why don't we go on Saturday, would that be all right with you?"

"All right, Dad, we can go Saturday. Goodnight," Chris said in a tight sounding voice.

Brian put his arms around his son and kissed him. "Goodnight." It was all he could say as his own throat had tightened up too.

Tom had another drink ready for Brian when he sat down again after talking to Chris. There was a far away look in his eyes.

"You were telling me last night about your uncle who did guiding around Canal Flats; does he still do it?" Tom thought it would be good to get Brian's mind on something else until Chris was sleeping, then he would try to help them unburden their minds of the events of the day.

"He gave it up after a few years. He couldn't stand how some of them treated his horses, and then he had a few bad experiences. He still gets furious when he tells about this one smartass who shot at a cougar and wounded it for no reason at all. The cougar went into a cave, and Uncle Albin had to go in and destroy it since you know how dangerous it is having a wounded cougar roaming around. It was a pretty hair-raising experience being in a dark cave with a wounded animal that could spring on you at any moment. Things like that finally made him give it up, but he had some very rewarding experiences as well. We should get together with him sometime; I'm sure you two would enjoy each other."

"I'm sure we would, Brian, and I'd love to meet him sometime."

There was a lull in the conversation, and Jennifer noticed that Tom kept glancing toward Christopher's bunk. She got up and went over to check on him and found that he was in the very deep sleep that comes to a child who has exhausted himself crying for a long period of time.

"He's sound asleep," she said as she sat down again in her chair by the fire.

Tom filled the stove with wood and then leaned back and cleared his throat.

"I had the feeling that something more happened to upset you two today than losing the ram. Do you want to talk about it, or should I mind my own business?"

Jennifer looked at Brian and hoped he would talk to Tom about what happened at the scene of the ram fight rather than harbour his feelings like he usually did. But she needn't have worried. There was something about Tom and being in a cabin by the fire in the mountains that helped Brian unleash his inhibitions.

"Yeah, no, it's okay, Tom." Brian raised his hand to stop Tom who was obviously going to apologize for having spoken out of turn. "We should talk about it and get it out of our systems. It came as a shock to both Jennifer and me to learn that Chris thought that Sam could lead him to heaven where his mother is, and he could ask her to come back."

"Jennifer mentioned this morning that his mother had died, but that's incredible."

"I knew he was up to something pretty important to him, that's why I consented to the trip. I was worried about him when he seemed to turn against Jennifer and decided the best way to solve the problem was to go along with his wishes. I didn't want any rifts between Jennifer and Chris. This family has had enough heartache. And although it has been a painful experience for all of us, it seems to have worked out. I think it has brought us closer together." Brian smiled at Jennifer.

"He loves Jennifer, you can see that," Tom said. "The poor

185

little guy must have been very confused thinking his mother could come back and trying to love Jennifer at the same time."

"He was," Jennifer said, "but he sobbed it all out today, and he let me comfort him. That's what's important. I thought I had failed, that I had done something to hurt him," Jennifer resolved to have more confidence in herself.

"It was my fault; I should have made things clear to him when it all happened, but he was pretty small then," Brian said.

"You can't blame yourself, Brian," Tom said, "Who knows what's the right thing with children. But where did he ever get such a notion?"

"His mother loved the ram and he did too. We thought it was a symbol of new life that the ram came the day Chris was born. Joanne referred to him as 'Christopher's Sam' and so he naturally associated the ram with her. Sam went away to the mountains, and his friend's mother said that mountains touch heaven. I told him his mother had gone to heaven. So he just put it all together and thought Sam came up here to heaven to see his mother, and all he had to do was follow Sam and he could see her too," Brian said.

"Besides, he had the idea which children often do when there is a death in the family, that she went away because he was bad. I nearly went to pieces today when he told me that he wanted to ask her to forgive him. I hope I convinced him that it had nothing to do with him, and that his mother loved him dearly," Jennifer ended with a note of sadness in her voice.

"I'm sure you did, Jennifer. He seemed fine tonight, and look at the way he's sleeping. He sure is a stout-hearted boy. Sometimes when he's talking he sounds so mature, one forgets he's only a child. But I suppose that comes from growing up on a ranch, so close to nature," Tom said.

"And the fact that he spends a lot of time with his father," Jennifer added, without resentment. "It was one of the things that attracted me to him when we met, how strong he is." How strong they both are, she thought as she looked at Brian with her love shining in her eyes.

Tom saw the look that Jennifer gave Brian and sighed with envy. Then he said, "That ram still interests me. I'm not really into the zodiac stuff, but I have read a little bit about it up here for something to do. When did you say he came to your ranch?"

"I've been thinking about that myself. I don't really believe in these things. Joanne did a bit. If Chris hadn't been born late, he would have been born under the sign of the ram. He was born on May first and the ram came that day and stayed. Another thing about it that I can never get out of my mind is that Joanne nearly bled to death when Chris was born, and when I went home the ram was there nearly bleeding to death also. It's incredible when you think about it."

"Hard to believe," Tom said in awe. "But those sheep are different from most wild animals somehow. I think that's why they fascinate us so much. They seem to be surrounded by mystery. It was very unusual for anyone to get as close to a ram fight as you did today. The sheep I've seen have all been at a distance, but I'd give a lot to watch a ram fight."

"I'm sure it was because Sam knew us that we got that close and, of course, he was herding the ewes by the time we got there so they stayed with him. The other ram came because the ewes were there. It was some experience for us. Too bad Sam got killed," Brian said.

"They don't live very long anyway. They fight over the ewes until they are so exhausted they can't eat. They get weak, and some other animal gets them so that they can survive. It's just a case of animal eat animal in the wilderness. The foliage-eating ones feed the carnivorous ones. It's a vicious circle. You say it was painful for Chris to learn as he did about life and death. But I think children accept things, especially natural things, better than we do.

"I think it was a good place for him to learn. You are just feeling bad because you think you didn't explain to him about his mother, but I think kids get ideas like this no matter what we do. And we blame ourselves because we are conditioned by society to do that," Tom said, and he looked at Brian to see if his words were helping to relieve him, and saw that Brian was lost in thought.

He looked at Jennifer and saw that she was watching Brian's face intently. Tom knew then that there was more keeping these two people from happiness than their concern over Christopher and wondered what it could be. They loved each other, that was obvious. Life has less complications when one gets older, he thought; that is the consolation, and he sighed audibly. Brian and Jennifer both looked at him so he said, "I'm going out to pick up some kindling I chopped for morning."

Tom put on his jacket and opened the door. He was greeted by a starlit sky that nearly took his breath away by its beauty. He turned to Brian and Jennifer with a smile.

"Whether you believe in astrology or not, there is a good chance to see of the signs of the zodiac out here tonight."

Brian was out of his chair in a flash, "Let's see if we can find the constellation that forms the first sign in the zodiac, the ram." He grabbed his jacket on his way out of the door.

And Jennifer was right behind him. Tom handed her jacket to her as she went by him. "It's cold out; there's going to be a heavy frost tonight," he said as he followed, closing the door behind him.

Jennifer filled her lungs with cold crisp mountain air, so different from the soft sea air she was used to in Vancouver, and said, "It's absolutely beautiful. I've never seen anything like it before."

"How could you? In Vancouver you can't even see the stars." Brian never missed an opportunity to let her know how much better off she was since he rescued her or something like that.

"There's the big dipper." Tom was pointing off into the sky. "Where?" Jennifer asked. "I've never seen it." But as much as Tom pointed and tried to direct her gaze, she couldn't see anything in the sky that looked like a dipper to her. Brian was laughing at her, but he came over and stood behind her and pointed to the sky with his arm resting on her shoulder.

"See that star right above my finger?"

"Yes."

"And the next one," he said.

"Yes." And a few minutes later as Brian traced the handle of the big dipper for her she saw the whole thing and said thrilled, "Oh, I see it, I see it now."

"All right, now look up from the two stars that form the front of the dipper, see that bright star up there?" Brian asked, still pointing over her shoulder.

"Yes," she said, loving the closeness of his body to hers.

"That's the North Star."

"Oh, this is fun; you know I never really believed you could see them without using a lot of imagination. Do either of you know where Aries is? I have this feeling that Sam is up there watching us," Jennifer said with a note of sadness.

"I have always felt, and Joanne did too, that Sam watched over Chris, but I don't know where to find Aries, do you, Tom? I was hoping you did."

"No, I don't, but there is the bear over there."

Tom and Brian had a contest then to see who could recognize the most stars in the constellation and pointed them out to Jennifer, who after a little practice could see them without any difficulty. Then the moon came into full view from behind a mountain peak and dimmed the galaxy.

"I don't remember seeing so many stars as we did tonight," Tom said as they walked towards the cabin door after he picked up his kindling for the morning fire.

"I don't think I have, either. Boy, it's cold," Brian said as he grabbed Jennifer and put his cold hand down the back of her neck.

"Oh, Brian, you're mean," she said, laughing.

Silver arrived at the door to be let in for the night after spending the evening prowling the bush around the cabin.

Tom stoked up the fire, and Brian said, "Let's have one more drink for old times' sake."

"Good idea," Tom was all for that.

When they were all seated around the stove again with their steaming mugs of fragrant rum, they drank a series of toasts. To good luck, to good health, to their friendship, and to meeting again after Tom promised to visit them at Windsong. Tom banked the fire as best he could as the night promised to be a cold one. Then they crawled into their sleeping bags as they planned to get up early so the Logans could get a good start on their long journey home. It wasn't long until Tom's snoring competed with the crackling of the fire for dominance over the stillness that filled the cabin.

Brian was waiting for blessed sleep to release him from his anguished thoughts. He was dreading the time when he would have to tell Chris about his mother's illness. How long did he have, he wondered, now that Chris had started school, before some child unwittingly told Chris about the time Joanne had become disoriented, when Chris was a baby. It had been talked about all around the small community of Golden.

Brian's face burned with shame when he thought of how angry he had been when he came home from school, and found her gone, with Chris, and her purse left sitting on the table.

He had been impatient with her depressions all along, telling her that she was only giving in to weakness. Postpartum blues was all in the mind.

Just the night before when he had come home, Chris was sitting on the kitchen floor playing with his toys, and Joanne was in the bedroom lying on the bed crying.

"What's the matter?" Brian had asked. "Why are you crying again?" Annoyance sounded in his voice. He was tired and hungry. There were no preparations for dinner when he walked through the kitchen.

She turned to face him and her face was all red and puffy, indicating that she had been crying for some time. "I don't know." She had answered in an unhappy voice.

"Joanne, what do you mean, you don't know? You must be crying for a reason, people don't just cry for nothing." But she cried harder for a time while he stood there helplessly watching her. "It's not unusual for women to have depression after they have had a baby, you know. But you just refuse to believe that it can happen." She had flung the words at him with contempt.

"Well, are you going to get up and make some dinner? Chris must be getting hungry, it's time he ate, isn't it?"

She had got up then, and threw together a makeshift dinner, which they ate in silence.

He thought that she had left like this to show him that he was wrong. But when she didn't return he became worried and started making enquiries. He learned from a mill worker in

Donald that he had seen her driving out of town at about three in the afternoon, heading west. And yes, Chris was with her, he had seen the baby sitting in his car seat in the back.

She had just up and left without knowing what she was doing, until she found herself in Salmon Arm, with no money and a baby, with no milk or diapers. She phoned her mother in Vancouver, who arranged for her to be accommodated in Salmon Arm for the night and then to continue on to Vancouver the next day.

Madeline informed Brian of the arrangements when he called her, after learning that Joanne had been seen heading west. Madeline had convinced him to take the bus to Vancouver, and they could straighten things out when he got there, which he did.

Joanne had been right as rain when he arrived, so they spent an enjoyable weekend together, dining and dancing, while Madeline looked after her cherished grandson. So it was decided that Joanne had been homesick for her family, and that she should stay for a visit, which she did.

Brian went home to Golden to his teaching job. He flew out to Vancouver two weeks later and brought them home. Their life together was good again for a time. But it was only the beginning of the nightmare that was to follow. It was the first time that Brian had come close to admitting that Joanne was ill. He would not accept it, even after Joanne herself had accepted that she had become incurably ill. She wrote about it in her journal, in hopes that others afflicted with the disease would benefit from what she had learned in her efforts to overcome it.

It wasn't until after she had died that Brian knew she had no control over her illness or its effects upon her, and it pained him deeply. Now he wished that he had understood, and been more of a comfort to her.

His weakness smote him, and he recalled a Shakespearean style of play he had seen while attending UBC, that had left him with the feeling that he was a fraud, not a man. He hadn't paid full attention to the dialogue, as he was still in mourning, and kept drifting into his own thoughts, but the scenario had somehow touched off his feelings of incompetence.

The actors were wearing long white robes. They had their backs to Brian at first, and he couldn't make out what they were saying. There were two men talking and their voices sounded familiar to him. When they turned around, they looked like his grandfather and his father. The voice that sounded like his grandfather said, "It was an omen; the sun is the symbol of strength; Christopher is the protector of travelers." When the lights dimmed, the head of the actor who looked like his grandfather had turned into a ram, and the ram said, "Christopher followed his symbol, the ram, to its death; old wounds were opened and cleaned." The actor who looked like his father also had the head of a ram, and he said, "There is healing of the old wounds, and new life, new life for the searchers."

And now Brian's son Christopher had followed his ram to its death; what a coincidence it was. The words from the play came back to him again, "Old wounds were opened and cleaned." Well, old wounds had certainly been opened this day, he thought, and he hoped they were cleaned, and that there would be healing, and a new life for them all, as yes, they were "the searchers."

A coyote's howl off in the wilderness reminded Brian of the lateness of the hour, and that they had a long ride home tomorrow. He turned over in his bunk and willed himself to sleep.

15   The Journey Home

They awoke in the morning to the sound of Christopher laughing and Silver barking. Brian sat up and asked, "What's going on?"

"A mouse ran across the floor and Silver tried to catch it." Chris was highly amused by the scene he claimed to have witnessed.

When Jennifer heard what Chris said, she was glad she was in the top bunk as she didn't have much use for mice.

Tom was a heavy sleeper but the ruckus woke him up too, and he wanted to know what had awakened everybody. Chris managed to stop laughing long enough to say, "A mouse just ran into Jennifer's boot."

Jennifer sat bolt upright at that, "It did not."

"Yes, it did," Chris went into another fit of laughter at the look of horror on Jennifer's face.

"Chris, are you playing a trick on Mom?" Brian asked, trying to sound stern.

"No, Dad, honest, look, Silver is trying to get it out."

And sure enough Silver was whining and scratching at Jennifer's boot. Brian got up and took the boot to the door and Silver followed. He opened the door, and a cold draft of morning air bust into the room. As Brian tipped up the boot a fat little mouse fell to the ground and scurried to the protection of the bushes nearby, Silver pounced after it but missed. Jennifer, who had witnessed the event, shrieked, "I won't wear them, I won't." And that sent Chris off into another peal of laughter. Brian and Tom joined in the laughter as well.

As Jennifer felt a wave of morning sickness hit her as a result of the wretched mouse, she hoped with all her heart that she would have a daughter to join her in defence against these merciless men.

The fire from the night before had burned to a heap of cold ashes in the stove. Tom started a fresh fire, and by the time the Logans had their belongings packed the smell of coffee filled the air. They all sat down to the hearty breakfast prepared by Tom.

After breakfast, Tom offered to feed and water the horses while the Logans put the finishing touches to their packing. Chris hastened to offer his assistance to Tom as he wanted to have a few minutes alone with his friend before they left. And Tom readily accepted his offer, sensing that the boy had something on his mind.

They were leading the horses down to the river to drink when Chris said, "We're coming back in the spring to see Sam's babies, Tom. Will you be here then?"

"Yes, I'll be here."

"And can we stay with you again?"

"Yes, you can stay with me. I'd enjoy having you."

"And will you go with us to see the baby lambs? I'll show you where Sam's buried, if you do."

"If I can I will," Tom said, wondering what Chris was leading up to.

"My Dad is going to show me where my mother's grave is." Chris stifled a little sob, and then continued, "I wanted to ask her to come home, but she can't come back, Tom, neither can Sam. You can't come back when you're dead. Did you know that? It's final. Dad says it's final."

"Yes, Chris, that's how it is." Tom saw the tears gathering in Christopher's eyes, and understood his need to discuss his loss with him, after such a cruel fact of life had so suddenly been thrust upon him. And he prayed inwardly that he would be able to guide Chris into acceptance of these seemingly brutal truths that we cannot change.

"So in a way it was like losing your mother yesterday, too, wasn't it?" Tom asked in a kindly voice.

"Yes," Chris said with tears in his voice, then after gaining control of his emotions he continued, "I miss her."

"I know just how you feel, Chris. I lost my own mother when I was quite young and I know how hard it is to accept." Tom reached out and put his hand on Christopher's shoulder as if to steady him.

Chris had felt that Tom would be able to help him cope with the sorrow that he was holding inside. And here was Tom telling him that it had happened to him too. When Chris looked up and saw the warmth and understanding in Tom's face he felt a deep affection for this kindly outdoor man.

"It hurts lots, Tom, doesn't it?"

"Yes, it hurts lots, Chris, but time heals, you know. You have to be strong like I know you already are, and you have to give these things time. And when you do you will learn to put your feelings in their proper place, and you will feel better."

"Will my stomach ache go away then? It makes me feel awful sick." Chris put his hand on his stomach as if to see if the ache was gone already.

"Yes, it will go away, and you will be able to remember only the happy times you had with your mother, and with Sam. You'd like that, wouldn't you, Chris?"

"Yes, I liked it when she laughed at the funny things Sam did. But when I think of her going away in her car it makes me cry."

"Well then, you have to stop thinking about the things that make you cry and think only about the good times. And by doing that the hurt will go away."

"That's what I'm going to do, Tom."

Tom heard the determination in Christopher's voice and saw that the worried look had left his face, and he was pleased. This boy certainly had the makings of a fine young man, he thought.

As they were leading the horses back to the cabin to be

saddled, Tom said, "You just remember to keep your chin up, Chris, and let time do the rest."

"Thanks, Tom, I will," Chris said as he gave Tom a big smile to show him that he meant it.

Jennifer put on her boots after Brian had turned them both upside down and run his hand up inside to prove to her that there were no more mice in them. She knew they would be telling that one on her for years, and thought that somebody had to supply them with laughter.

Tom helped Brian with the horses, and as Chris and Jennifer emerged from the cabin they had them waiting at the door. Nelliebell was carrying their packs again, but she looked refreshed after her day's rest. It had been a frosty night as Tom had predicted, and the horses' breath looked like monsters snorting steam in the cold morning light.

The Logans lingered, expressing their thanks to Tom for his generous hospitality before bidding him a fond farewell. And then rode off down the hiking trail where they had stumbled along in the falling snow only two short nights before. Those few days now seemed like a whole lifetime to the riders.

As they approached the first bend in the trail, Jennifer turned when she heard Tom call to her.

"Jennifer, you ride like you were born in the saddle," Tom said, laughing as he waved goodbye.

Jennifer waved and said, "Thanks, Tom," and then rode around the bend out of sight, leaving Tom Shannon and the wardens' station behind. It had been an experience she would never forget, and she had high hopes that it would benefit them all. She knew she had learned a lot on this sojourn in "Brian's hills," about life, about herself, and about the two people she loved most in all the world, who were riding down the trail ahead of her to Windsong and home.

Jennifer was prepared for Bess to balk when they came to the place where they had crossed the river with Tom when his horse had slipped on the rocks. When she felt her hesitate she held the reins tight and gave her a nudge in the flank, and Bess crossed the river without any further hesitation behind Chris and Jingle. She saw Brian turn his head to see if she needed

196

help, and then finding that she didn't, he gave an approving nod before riding on. Although it wasn't much, she knew it meant that she had passed the test of horsemanship as far as he was concerned, and that meant a lot.

They pushed the horses hard that first day down the Otterhead River on the way back, as they had been away longer than they had expected to be, and there were obligations waiting for them at home.

Jennifer was surprised at the change in scenery the earth had undergone in the short time since they passed that way following Sam. The trees and shrubs had shed the last remnants of their summer attire and stood naked waiting for the white fleece to dress them for the long winter's night. She wondered if the wind and snow had hastened the process of the changing seasons, as the leaves that had rustled under the horses' feet were now brown and dank with a musty smell that rose to assail their nostrils as they passed by.

They followed the same route taken by Sam on the way up, and only stopped when it was necessary to rest the horses and eat a sandwich for lunch. They crossed Porcupine Creek and then Glenogle Creek, but avoided the ravine where the slide had occurred. And then they stopped on a ridge to rest the horses and remove their jackets.

"See that rugged peak that stands out above the rest?" Brian said, pointing east. "That's where we were. The Otterhead River runs at the foot of that mountain."

"I can't believe we were that high; no wonder it's so much warmer down here," Jennifer said, surprised.

"That's where Sam's grave is, too, isn't it?" Chris said gravely.

"Yes, near there, Chris," Brian said. There was silence as they stood, remembering.

It was the first time Chris had mentioned Sam since telling Tom about losing him the night before, and Jennifer was surprised that a child so young could handle his emotions so well. If he had shed any more tears over the loss of his beloved animal and the disappointment in not being able to see his mother, he had done it when no one was there to see. Understanding about his mother seemed to have brought acceptance of her to Chris. He was more like the little boy she had enjoyed when she first came to Windsong. She wondered what his reaction would be to the empty corral near the barn where Sam had spent most of his time.

But soon there would be Christmas to occupy his mind and the new baby to look forward to. It thrilled her to think that they would soon be home, and she would find an opportunity to tell first Brian and then Chris the wonderful news about the baby. But the thrill ebbed when she thought of how Brian had withdrawn into himself, and she knew he was consumed with guilt over Joanne's death. It was the obstacle to be hurdled for them to find a measure of happiness now that Christopher's affection for her was returning. It will take time, she thought; you can't push Brian, he goes at his own pace.

As they rode on in the lazy afternoon, Chris became bored and asked Jennifer if she would sing, but this time there was no rancour in his voice.

"What would you like to hear? Humpty-Dumpty?" she said, pleased that he had asked her.

Chris laughed and then said, "I really like that scout song, 'cause it's where we are."

"Okay, but how about you singing it with me?"

"I don't know it."

"Then I'll teach it to you."

As Jennifer taught Chris to sing, Brian thought how right Chris was; it really is like the words in the song. Her sweet rich voice rang out in the clear mountain air:

Land of the silver birch, home of the beaver
Where still the mighty moose wanders at will.
Blue lake and rocky shores I will return once more
Boom diddy boom boom, boom diddy boom boom, boom diddy boom boom boom.
My heart is sick for thee, here in the low lands I will return to thee, hills of the north.
Refrain.
Swift as the silver fish, canoe of birch bark
By mighty waterways carry me forth.

198

Refrain.
There where the blue lake lies I'll set my wigwam
Close to the water's edge, silent and still.
Refrain.

After they sang several of Christopher's favorite songs, Brian turned in the saddle with a request of his own on his lips when Jennifer started to hum the first familiar notes of "The Way We Were," the song he was about to request. She reads my mind, he thought, as her voice crescendoed into volume and the words of the song broke forth from her lips. I'll have to give her a bad time about those little freckles on the bridge of her nose that she is so self-conscious about. He smiled to himself at the pleasure of his thoughts.

The animals that inhabited the area were treated to a rare serenade that day, as Jennifer had a strong well-trained voice that was a pleasure to hear. Chris joined Jennifer again, and they would no sooner finish one song than they would start on another, and so they went on and on. They rode for miles over rocks and ridges, down ravines and valleys, and across creek after creek on their way back to Windsong after their journey into the heart of the Rocky Mountains.

While Chris and Jennifer whiled away the hours in the warm afternoon singing songs, Brian became deeply lost in thought. When he was telling Tom the night before about Chris getting rid of his guilt feelings, he remembered that his own guilt was not all connected to the rift between Chris and Jennifer.

He had a rotten feeling in the pit of his stomach. He remembered Madeline, Joanne's mother, saying, "You're living in the past, Brian, when you have a chance to be happy. You're waiting for yesterday to return." Dear, sweet, understanding Madeline, who wanted to see Chris and himself have a good life. Brian recalled her saying, when he told her he was going to marry Jennifer, "That girl has a lot of love to give. She has a strong maternal instinct that will develop when she has a family and a place of her own. She will make you a good home." Madeline was a strong believer that everyone should have a good home. It was a necessity of life as far as she was concerned, but how was he going to be happy when he had this rotten feeling of guilt in his gut that he couldn't get rid of. Only he knew the reason for his regrets, as he had never been able to tell anyone. After the singing died away, there was very little conversation exchanged by the three riders on the first day of their descent to civilization. Each seemed to be lost in the secret traces of their own minds and in the beauty of the surroundings, whose tranquility gave heir to the soul-searching thoughts in which each was engaged.

Most of Christopher's silence on the way home was because he was trying to learn to put his feelings in their proper place, as Tom had said he should. He was preparing himself for a life at Windsong without Sam. And to live with the knowledge that his mother was never coming back. That was a large undertaking for a young boy.

He still felt like crying when he thought of her, but Tom had said, "It will all heal in time. Keep your chin up." And that was what he was going to do. He was going to keep his chin up. He had said Sam's name already without crying. And if animals live on in their offspring like Dad said they did, and if Sam had a son, he would find his way to Windsong to live, he was sure of it. And that thought made him feel a whole lot better.

He missed Sam terribly, and he thought of the little lambs that would be born in the spring, which might look like Sam. But mostly he thought about getting back to school and all the exciting things he had to tell, now that he had been on a big trip into the wilderness. He would be able to boast about being all the way to the Yoho National Park and back by horse. None of his friends had done that; they had all just gone fishing or camping in their families' campers.

Jennifer was thinking about death and trying to understand the reason for the remorse she had seen in Brian's suffering eyes when he told her about Joanne's death. She saw it again after Tom had told him not to feel guilty about Chris. She saw him withdraw into that inner chamber of thought he would not share with her. She had never experienced losing someone close to her, and had no way of knowing what it was like. She had read that people feel guilty when someone they love dies, and that it was more difficult when there was a suicide.

After Sam died she knew that Brian, as well as Chris, had been hanging on to Joanne through Sam. Now she suspected there was more to it than that with Brian. He had some personal reason for his feelings of guilt and wished that he could understand that no person has jurisdiction over life and death, only destiny handles such immense decisions.

Suddenly Jennifer understood about Gail. She hadn't got over losing Joanne either. She was hanging on to her through Brian and Chris. Although she had brought them together, when it came to the reality of a wedding she hadn't been able to face up to it because she had never put her sister's death in its place. Now that she understood her friend, Jennifer knew that she loved her still. Now that she understood all of them better, her love for them was less inhibited. For a minute Jennifer wished she could instill what she had learned about life on their journey in the mountains into her unborn child. Then she knew she wouldn't rob her child of the reward that tough experience brings.

Jennifer looked at Brian riding ahead with the lead from the pack horse in one hand resting on his thigh, and the rein from Glory in the other. She wondered what thoughts he had engaged to torture himself with, as he had a slight stoop to his shoulders. She had learned that he replaced the proud Logan carriage she had come to love with a slight stoop when he was burdened.

Jennifer would have been shocked at the depth of self-torture Brian was inflicting on himself at that moment.

Only a man like Brian Logan, raised to shoulder responsibility for his wife and family, could understand the blame he was attaching to himself in the loss of the first girl he had ever loved and the mother of his child.

He was so full of responsibility for everything that had happened to his family that he unknowingly placed himself in the position of being responsible for the course of other people's lives. Fate of such things is attributed by most to be in the hands of a greater power than man. Brian was so lost in self-blame that he could see nothing else. Ever since Joanne died he had looked at only what he wanted to see. He had managed to bury himself in the duties of his teaching position and Christopher's needs. But when Sam died and Chris demanded an explanation of things, the self-incrimination he had managed to submerge reared its ugly head to plague him and he was again burdened with regrets. And now he knew that even when he married Jennifer he hadn't been honest with himself.

16 Due for Good News

When they came within earshot of Hospital Falls, Jennifer knew where they were. But it seemed to her that they must still have a long way to go to reach Windsong, as it was the second morning of their journey up the mountain that they had stopped at the falls.

"Brian, it seems to me that we're still a long way from home, and it's already late afternoon. Are we going too slow?"

"No, it's not that far. It's just that Sam took the long way around, going along the Kicking Horse and then up Dark Creek. It was as if he was heading to one place and then changed his mind and went to another. It will be faster to get to Windsong by following Hospital Creek to North Bench. And actually, we've been making darned good time," Brian said.

They didn't stop at the falls but kept on going. Below the falls they came to a low area where the creek overflows its banks when the snow melts in the spring. The vegetation was almost tropical in its density, and the horses' feet sank into the soft depth of humus accumulating for decades on the forest floor. The tall timbers so outstripped the bushes in growth that they were spreading everywhere, groping for a glimpse of sunlight. The abundant growth of ferns was still green at that altitude. It was dark and damp and the odor of decaying vegetation permeated the air. Jennifer was relieved when they passed through the area into the open again. But the long shadows of early evening were beginning to fall, and the travelers were aware that Indian summer was drawing to a close. The sun would soon be gone, leaving the mountains to the chill of an autumn night.

Jennifer caught sight of a stump on the side of the trail so rotted with age it was supporting a layer of green moss from which some ferns were growing. Nature expressing growth, she thought, the continuance of life through growth, the old rotting stump supporting the growth of moss and fern. Nature wastes nothing. Then she became absorbed in thought of the wastefulness of man with only the sound of the horses' hooves in the soft earth and the creak of the leather saddles to disturb her.

Brian looked over his shoulder and saw that Chris and Jennifer were lagging behind. He watched their slow hesitant progress and noted that the horses were responding to the mood of the riders and realized that he too was getting tired. They had put in a long hard day's ride, and had covered a lot of ground.

"I think we'd better try to make it to higher ground before we make camp. If we can just hang on until we reach that next ridge we'll be out of the heavy fog that will cover this swamp as soon as the sun goes down," Brian called to Chris and Jennifer.

"All right, keep going," Jennifer called back. "We're fine, aren't we, Chris?"

"Can't we make it home tonight, Dad?"

"No, it's a bit too far, no use taking a chance of having one of the horses stumble in the dark and get injured. We'll be home by noon tomorrow, or earlier if we get up early."

They rode on in silence and came to the crest of the ridge in time to see the last red glow of the sun on the sky above the mountains to the west. They made camp on the ridge above Hospital Creek. Chris wanted to set up the campfire, so Jennifer decided to help Brian unsaddle the horses. Now that she had learned how to ride and loved it, she decided it was time she learned how to saddle and tend to a horse.

When they finished unsaddling the horses, Brian took them down to the creek to water while Jennifer went to give Chris a hand setting up camp. She found he had done an excellent job and had a nice fire started. After Chris declined her offer of assistance in gathering wood to keep the fire going, Jennifer started off for the creek to join Brian.

The thought of even a few minutes alone with him beckoned her after the closeness of the quarters they had been sharing the past few days with Chris and Tom. In her haste to reach Brian's side before he started to return to camp, she made the error of going down the steep side of the bank, rather than the longer, more gentle slope Brian had taken. Jennifer had one more thing to learn about the mountains and that was the danger of wet moss on smooth rocks. When she stepped on such a rock, both feet went out from under her and she fell the remainder of the way down the bank and landed almost at Brian's feet, as a wave of darkness overcame her.

Brian dropped the horses' reins and ran to aid Jennifer. When he saw she was on the verge of losing consciousness, he quickly stripped off his shirt and dipped it in the creek to sponge her face and neck. "Jennifer, what the hell is going on?" he asked with fear in his voice. And when he saw that she was coming to, he put his arm around her shoulders and lifted her to a sitting position.

"I fell," she said, as a wave of nausea hit her, and she leaned over in a fit of retching from an empty stomach.

"Have you broken something?" Brian started feeling her legs and arms for any signs of broken bones.

"No, I don't think so," she said, between the misery of heaving.

"What's making you sick then?" he asked in alarm.

Seeing the look of fear on his face and feeling the wretchedness of her nausea, she cried out her secret, "I'm pregnant."

"My God, are you sure?" he asked, taking both her hands in his. And when she nodded yes, he cupped his hand in the creek and let her drink the icy water from his hand. He did that several times and sponged her face again. When her retching stopped he asked, "Do you think you have hurt anything?"

"No," she said, giving him a wan smile to relieve the look

of alarm on his face. He took her in his arms then and kissed her face.

"I'm just thrilled about the baby," he said reassuringly.

But Brian didn't feel thrilled; he felt badly shaken by her announcement of another responsibility when he was at the nadir of self-respect for failing to care for the ones he already had. He was suffering miserably over his neglect of Chris, which was revealed when Sam died, and his failure in preventing Joanne's tragic death. He was trying hard to sound pleased that Jennifer was pregnant as he did not want her to know that her news had come at a very inopportune time for him.

"But why didn't you tell me?" he asked.

"I only found out on Friday, and since then there just hasn't been a chance."

She felt better as the cold water settled her stomach and she was sure she had not hurt herself seriously.

"How far along is it?"

"About two months; it's due some time in June."

He felt better now that he knew Jennifer was not hurt.

"What a way to tell a guy he's going to be a father, come tumbling down the bank and landing at his feet! I think you should go in for a check as soon as we get home."

"But I'm all right, dear."

"Just the same, I think you should make sure. We'll call the doctor as soon as we get home and see what he says, anyway."

"If you insist," she sighed, "but I'm sure I'm all right; it's just that I hit my funny bone when I fell and skinned my shin, I was getting weak and hungry."

"I'm going to insist, but right now we'd better get you up to the camp and have some supper."

Chris had come to the top of the bank to see what was keeping them, and seeing Jennifer on the ground he yelled in alarm, "What's happened to Jennifer, is she hurt?" A note of concern entered his voice.

"She's all right, Chris," Brian called back, "We're coming up right now."

Then he turned to Jennifer and asked, "Do you think we should tell him about the baby?"

"Why not? I think he's due for some good news after what he went through yesterday. Don't you?"

"You're right about that; do you feel well enough to go back now?"

"Yes." She got up with Brian's help and walked shakily back to camp. When Brian and Jennifer reached the camp, Chris had a roaring fire going and a pot of water boiling in case they wanted to have a hot drink, he said. He knew the ways of camping out and had everything in shape. Silver was lying by the fire as if pleased with his young master's accomplishment.

"Speaking of a drink," Brian said, "I think I might just have enough for us each to have one for a celebration."

"What are we celebrating?" Chris asked when Brian handed him his usual portion of a few drops drowned in hot water and honey.

"Jennifer has a nice surprise," he said as he gave her a proud smile.

"What is it, Jennifer?" Chris asked, and hoped it wasn't that he could miss school tomorrow if they got home by noon, as he was planning on going for the afternoon. He couldn't wait until the next day to tell about his trip to the mountains.

"You're going to have a baby sister or brother in the spring," Jennifer said, in happy anticipation of his excitement. She laughed when she saw his eyes get as big as saucers.

"Really?" Chris said excitedly.

"Yes, really."

"Boy oh boy, that's super! Yippee! Yippee!" Chris jumped around the camp with glee, and then stopped to tell Silver. "I'm going to have a sister! What's her name going to be?" he asked Jennifer when he stopped hopping around.

"It could be a brother, you know, and we have lots of time to pick out a name," Jennifer said, smiling.

"It's all right if it's a brother, but I'd like a sister best. Can I help think of her name?" he asked emphatically, as if by impressing Jennifer of his desire for a sister it may have some effect on the sex of the unborn child.

They drank their rum with several toasts to the new baby and to Jennifer, and ate their supper by the light of the campfire as darkness descended. They sat around in silence enjoying the fire as a chill had replaced the warmth in the air when the shadows deepened into night.

When Jennifer looked at Chris, he knew that she had seen his head start to nod. He got up without being told and said, "I'm going to bed. Goodnight."

"I'll tuck you in," Jennifer said. She waited a minute for him to get settled and then went to the tent to bid him good night. He reached out his arms to her, and she bent to receive the expected kiss, but he hugged her and said, "That's a bear hug. Goodnight, Mom."

When she looked at him, she saw that he was smiling and his dimples were showing.

"Goodnight, darling," she said with emotion, as the frustration of longing to hear him call her Mom again fell away, and she felt like a weight had been lifted off her shoulders. She wondered if Brian had heard, and when she returned to the fire and saw the pleased expression on his face, she knew that he had. But she thought his pleasure must be more for Chris than for her, as she didn't think Brian had any idea of the depth of her need to express her love for the child. A desire to be needed and to mother, and give, must have lain dormant inside her for years without her even knowing it was there. And now that it was released, it flowed in a torrent that wouldn't subside.

It was a good thing she was going to have two children to care for, she thought, or she would mother that one in the tent with the blond curls and dimpled smile too much. She thought about the baby coming and how she would fix up the third bedroom at Windsong into a nursery. She smiled at herself for turning into a mother hen that wanted to feather her nest, and wondered what her friends in the opera would think of her now. And then knew they would envy her, as they agreed it was wonderful to have a career, but it was also necessary to fulfil one's natural instincts as well. And after waiting so long to marry she didn't have many years left in which to experience the joys of motherhood. After Chris had gone to bed, Brian and Jennifer sat by the fire for a time, making plans for the new baby, and then decided to go to bed so that they could get an early start for home in the morning. The fire that Brian had banked for the night had burned itself to a heap of ash after being stirred by the rising wind long before the moon found its way to their camp on the ridge above Hospital Creek. The cover of the night gave a bobcat who roamed the area the courage to investigate their camp in search of food.

The rigorous pace of the trip had taken its toll on Silver, who usually kept guard, as well as on the Logans, and they had all fallen into a heavy, dreamless sleep. The bobcat was able to approach the camp and startle the horses who bolted, losing themselves in the rugged terrain before the dog awakened and sounded the alarm.

Brian, who was attuned to any change in circumstance in the outdoors was at the flap of the tent in a flash, rifle in hand. But as he looked out he discovered that the camp was in total darkness; he could see nothing. Only a few embers remained of the campfire he had banked with care, hoping it would last well into the night until the moon rose.

Silver was extremely upset and Brian could hear him bounding around the camp barking. The dog was used to the wilderness and did not sound the alarm needlessly.

Brian stepped stealthily from the tent, then raised his rifle to his shoulder and sent a shot volleying into the air. He suspected the night visitor to be a cat of some kind as there was no sound of a larger animal crashing through the bush when the shot rang out, and Silver left the camp in pursuit of the intruder. As Brian stood by the tent surrounded by the velvet darkness that enveloped their camp in the woods, he felt his skin start to crawl with the suspicion that something around him was out of place.

He recalled some of his Uncle Albin's experiences with mountain lions and wondered if there had been more than one invader of the night. He called Silver to return to help him in his investigation as well as for the dog's safety, as he had bounded off, heedless of care as he did sometimes when he was angry at having been caught napping. In his excitement the dog took a while to heed his master's command to return. By the time Silver was at Brian's side, pleading to be allowed to further pursue the offender of the night, Chris and Jennifer were at the tent flap demanding to know the cause of the ruckus and the welfare of Brian and Silver.

"Whatever it was has fled into the bush and won't be back after the chase Silver gave it," Brian said.

"What do you think it was?" Jennifer asked.

"Probably some kind of a small cat that would leave when a dog took after it. I'm glad we're out of the park so I can use my rifle," Brian said as he groped around in the dark for something to get the fire going, and then struck a match to some paper he had found and crumpled. It was a relief to them all to be able to see as the paper flared and Chris got the flashlight from the tent.

"There, that's better," Brian said. He grinned at Chris and Jennifer as they stepped gingerly from the tent and inched their way towards the fire while peering from side to side into the shadows. Brian's laughter died in his throat as he scanned the far reaches of the camp when the fire grew big enough to light the area, and Chris swept the light of the flash around. Jennifer and Chris followed Brian's silent gaze, and then Chris realized what was wrong and said in alarm, "The horses are missing."

"Oh no," Jennifer said, "What does that mean?"

"It means that if they don't find their way back we'll have to search for them in the morning." Brian sounded annoyed. He was trying to keep from alarming Jennifer and Chris, but it would mean a long walk to Windsong if the horses had gone home, and a long ride back to pick up their belongings.

"Can't we look for them tonight? The moon will soon be up." Chris sounded all enthused about going for the horses right then, although he knew it was not the thing to do, but he was anxious to get home.

"What we'd better do right now is get some sleep," Brian said, as he banked the fire for the second time. And they all went back to the tent to sleep for the remainder of the night.

The deep sleep that Jennifer had been enjoying before the rude awakening when Silver barked would not return. She kept going over the events of the past few days. She was pleased that Chris was turning to her again for love and affection. Now she knew it was his need for a mother's love that she had sensed and been drawn to when she and Brian were first married. Although Brian and his family were showing him affection, he missed his mother's love and she intended to meet his need as best she could. Now it was Brian's love she was seeking to make her life complete.

Whenever she saw his face while he was riding ahead of her down the mountain, she saw that he was deep in thought. She wished for a chance to speak to him about the burden he was carrying before they reached Windsong and returned to their busy lives. There had been very little opportunity for private conversation on the trip, and less chance for it in the morning with the need to find the horses and make up for lost time. She was getting restless and wondered if she dared slip from the tent and sit by the campfire, and then decided to do just that. The night was cool, so she stoked up the fire and zipped up her jacket; then she sat on a log with her back to the tent. She scanned the area where the firelight shone, satisfied that there was no danger lurking nearby. She returned to the thoughts that had kept her from sleep. She thought that both Brian and Chris were dead to the world and was startled when she heard Brian call softly behind her. She turned and saw him emerge from the tent in his socks and jacket.

"What are you doing out here all by yourself?" he asked.

"I couldn't go back to sleep and didn't want to wake you up so I came out here."

"I wasn't asleep. I thought you'd gone for a pee, and when you didn't come back I got worried. Then I saw the reflection of the fire on the tent and knew you had put on more wood. Getting pretty brave, aren't you, sitting out here all by yourself after we had a visit by a cat?"

"You said he wouldn't come back."

"No, he's not likely to after the chase Silver gave him," Brian said as he picked up a stick and started idly poking at the fire as he usually did when they sat by it at night.

To Jennifer it was the opportunity she had been waiting for, so she cleared her throat and looked at Brian. As she did so she longed to take him in her arms as she had Chris and kiss away

211

the depressed look she saw when she thought he was feeling guilty about Joanne.

"Last night I heard you tell Chris you would take him to the cemetary to see his mother's grave when he asked you to." Brian's face was unreadable, but she continued, "I think it's something you should do right away, before winter sets in, while she is on all our minds." She saw an unhappy look enter his eyes but he quickly masked it. "She is on your mind isn't she, Brian?" she asked softly, enticing him to speak. But he remained silent. "Brian, please talk to me about it." She reached out her hand and put it on his arm. "Why do you feel so guilty about it?" She waited for him to answer and when he didn't, she spoke again, as she was determined to get this thing out in the open for all their sakes, now that she had started speaking to him.

"The Forbes have accepted it. I think Gail has some mixed feelings about her sister's death, but the rest of them are going on with their lives, the way Joanne would want them to."

Seeing that she had brought him close to tears, she felt she had to press him while she had the chance. Besides, he was listening to her. He wasn't objecting to her questioning him like she had been afraid he would. "Why, darling? Why is it still hurting you so much?"

She was silent. Only the sound of the fire spitting on some wet wood and a coyote wailing off in the distance broke the stillness of the night.

Then he spoke hesitantly with a huskiness in his throat that she hadn't heard before.

"I don't know why." He couldn't tell her; he couldn't tell anyone, but he did know. He was silent for a few minutes and she waited for him to go on as she felt that he would, and he did. "I don't know why, because I failed, I guess." It was as close as he dared come to explaining it to her. Then like most men when they can't cope with their emotions he got angry and raised his voice. "Damn it, I should have been there to stop her, but I didn't know." His voice trailed off.

"But you were at the school. How could you have stopped

her? Nobody could have stopped her." She had raised her voice in her need to convince him.

Brian sat staring into the flames of the fire and watched them flare skyward. Each new attempt formed a different shape while the hot white and blue core of the flame tore at the pitch-covered logs. The same way that his remorse was eating at him, he thought, until he was good for nothing and it would never change, because he could not change the past. He recalled how Madeline's strength had helped him through their sorrow. "I can't despair," she said, "What good would that do? I'm needed. Christopher needs me to be strong. He needs you too, to be strong and to love him."

Yes, Brian thought, Chris needs me. He looked at Jennifer and wondered if she needed him. Jennifer was strong like Madeline, no wonder they got along so well. He needed her, he knew. Then he remembered she was pregnant and wondered if she would need him along the way, and if he would be able to fulfill that need. It seemed to him that he had never accomplished anything in his life. The son of a man who had been a Canadian war hero, and the grandson of a pioneer, who also was a giant of a man with a will of iron and nerves of steel.

When Jennifer saw that he was lost again in his own world, she decided she would say no more, but she must see that he kept his word to Chris. "Will you be taking Chris to the cemetery on Saturday?"

"Yes," he said, as he took her hand that had been resting on his arm in his, and drew her close to him.

"I only want to help; you're suffering needlessly."

He prevented her from saying more by kissing her long and lingeringly. Then he held her tightly against his chest and started running his hand through her hair, and whispered, "Let's go to bed."

Jennifer lay awake long after Brian appeared to have gone to sleep, wishing she could have said more to relieve Brian of his burden that was keeping them apart. Then she thought of her own part in all this. Her haste in pressing for a wedding date when she knew she wanted him.

Now she knew that you can't make someone love you by

getting married or by getting pregnant. It only obligates them to you. She knew she had been jealous of the mystery surrounding Joanne's death, and the understanding had brought shame. She had learned a lot on the trip and would keep on learning until she reached her goal of happiness for herself and her family. "Come hell or high water," she thought, with the will of wanting something badly enough. Jennifer's need for sleep overpowered her desire to think things out, and she fell into a deep relaxing sleep that is the reward of crisp mountain air.

The moon was up and shining before Brian went to sleep. There was enough light in the tent for him to see that Jennifer was sound asleep beside him. The serenity in her face made him want to kiss her, but he knew she needed rest and didn't want to risk waking her. He wondered if the baby would look like her, and hoped it would be a little girl with brown eyes and red-brown hair. Love for his unborn child stirred within him. He decided that he had been pretty lucky to meet Jennifer. He lay back to get more sleep and thought he should start counting his blessings instead of sheep. He nearly laughed out loud at the thought of counting sheep, as he knew that he had enough of sheep in the last few days to do him for a long, long time.

17   Strong Men

They were up in the morning as soon as it was light, which was not very early at that time of year. After a quick bite to eat and a hot coffee they were off in search of the horses. It took the Logans the better part of the morning to locate all four horses together over in the next ravine, it could have taken all day to find them if they had scattered. Chris kept saying he hoped they hadn't gone home. Jennifer shuddered at the thought of having to walk all the way to Windsong as she was stiff and sore from her fall down the bank the night before. It reminded her of the first morning on the trail when she had wakened to find she was stiff and saddle-sore, and was glad that being a greenhorn on a horse was behind her. They returned to camp with the horses and saddled up and loaded the pack horse for the last lap of the journey home.

They rode hard for the rest of the day without exchanging conversation except when necessary. Each rider was intent on the need to progress quickly in order to reach home without spending another night out on the trail. The sun's rays still held the warmth of Indian summer as they rode down the south fork of Hospital Creek to the junction with the north fork where they picked up a trail that was suitable for a four-wheel drive and great for the horses.

The trail wound around behind Mount Moberly, so named

for that famous pioneer who made his first camp at its foot when he was commissioned to explore the Selkirks.

Chris was so engrossed in all the things he had to tell at school, he didn't notice when they left Hospital Creek and climbed up to the bench. When he saw the old bootlegger's cabin in the trees above where they were riding, he knew they were getting close to home and he got excited.

"Can I phone Grandma right away and tell her all about our trip?"

"It's all right with me." Jennifer smiled at his need to tell his experience to his friends.

"Okay," Brian laughed.

Jennifer looked across the valley to the south west and caught her breath at it's beauty. "I see why they call those mountains the Dog Tooth Range, just look at those jagged peaks."

"Pretty nice, aren't they? That's where we'll be going heli-skiing."

"Is that where the Bugaboos are?"

"Right, and let's hope we can get enough snow while a pregnant lady can still ski." And he gave her a look that made her feel all warm inside. She, too, was getting excited about getting home. Brian had been looking at her all afternoon in a way that made her nerve ends tingle. The thought of the two of them being alone in their room after the affectionate way he had treated her the night before made her glow.

As they rode into the clearing above Windsong, the last bit of sun from the fading day was kissing the peaks of the Selkirk Mountains across the valley, and the river below was already swathed in shadow.

Jennifer's heart was bursting, a free and flying thing. Home, she thought, home is the sailor, home from the sea, and the searchers are home from the hills.

As they rode into the yard, Jennifer's excitement was marred as she looked toward the corral where Sam should be standing, giving them that curious superior look he had. She saw Chris glance that way and a look of sadness crossed his face, but he had things well under control and accepted the finality of it all. After he dismounted he set to helping Brian with the unsaddling of the riding horses and unloading the pack horse. As soon as Brian said he could handle the rest, he raced towards the house with Silver, who was showing his pleasure at being home by bounding excitedly around.

Jennifer gathered up what remained of their provisions, and by the time she entered the house Chris was well into the story of their trip on the phone with his Grandmother Logan. After he finished telling her everything he could think of, he phoned his Aunt Cheryl and repeated it all to her, until Jennifer had dinner ready and Brian told him it was time to eat.

The two men helped with the cleaning up after the meal and then started putting their camping gear away while Jennifer made their lunches for school. Chris even drew his own bath and spent a long time scrubbing without being told, and then called goodnight to them from the hall on his way to his room.

"I can't believe it; he went to bed without a fuss," Jennifer said to Brian. "He can't wait to get to school and tell the kids all about his trip. He's been listening to the others brag about their weekends for so long, and now it's his turn. And he thinks the sooner he goes to bed the sooner morning will come," Brian told her, sounding amused.

Jennifer was smiling as she went down the hall to tuck Chris in. The boy who had grown so big in size was only a child after all. He gave her a bear hug when she sat on his bed and leaned over to give him a goodnight kiss.

"Will I be able to hold the baby sometimes?"

"You sure will, in fact I'll be depending on you for help."

"I forgot to tell Grandma and Aunt Cheryl about the baby; can I go do it now?"

"I think it would be better if we told them on Sunday when we go for dinner. They probably want to kiss us and congratulate us, but you can do the telling, how's that?"

"Oh, yippee, that's super."

"Better go to sleep now, goodnight, honey."

"Night."

As Jennifer was leaving Christopher's room, she stopped at his dresser and looked at the pretty blonde girl smiling from the gold frame. She whispered softly only her lips moved, "Don't worry, Joanne, I'll take care of them."

For the remainder of the week after the Logans returned from tracking the ram, they were busy at work and getting caught up on the chores around Windsong. Then it was Saturday. The gift had been extended, but it was evident that Indian summer, although it had blessed them with an unusual amount of splendor, was drawing to a close. The sky was a pale blue and in the morning frost appeared. The haze was gone from the horizon, and the moon had lost its orange hue. A chilly wind blew down from the rocky peaks above and sang in the trees at Windsong. The sun rose a little later in the morning above the Rockies and set a little earlier behind the Selkirks, and the warmth of its rays had lost its intensity.

Brian got up early and went to the school to coach a basketball team. He was to be home for lunch and to take Chris to the cemetery. Each time Jennifer looked at the flowers on the dining room table for Chris to put on his mother's grave, she realized how much she was hoping that by going with Chris to visit Joanne's grave Brian would somehow come to understand that he couldn't have prevented the tragedy.

Chris had been in and out of the house for most of the morning and hadn't shown any anxiety until he came in for lunch, and then he chattered continuously.

"Are you coming to the cemetery with us?" he asked, sounding as if he wanted her along.

"No, dear, I'm not, but I'll be right here waiting for you to come home; how's that?"

"All right," Chris said.

Brian came home looking very restrained, and they all sat down to lunch.

"How did the game go this morning?" Jennifer asked.

"Good," Brian said curtly and then returned to his thoughts. There was silence at the table until Chris spoke.

"I saw a little brown rabbit over by the creek this morning. I bet it's the one that made those tracks in the snow last winter; 'member, Dad, when we found that path in the snow that went under the bushes where he lives?"

Jennifer looked at Brian, who hadn't answered Chris, and saw that he was so lost in thought that he hadn't heard a word Chris said.

"You mean you found where a little rabbit lives?" Jennifer asked.

"Yes, but we didn't disturb anything. We didn't look in his house to see if he was home, either."

"That's good. You wouldn't want to frighten him from his home in the wintertime; he might not find anywhere else to go."

Christopher's chattering was due to the nervous state he had worked himself into that morning while preparing himself for his visit to his mother's grave. He was determined not to cry. He wanted to show his father that he understood about life and death, and that he could accept things the way they are. He must remember that only her body was in the ground, and that her spirit, which was most important, was in heaven. She would live on through him, and he would remember her and love her forever.

They didn't talk any more after that. It was as if Brian's thoughts were so deep they commanded silence.

Nothing would have penetrated the depth of Brian's thoughts on that Saturday when he took Chris to the cemetery. He was wrestling with his own conscience, and conversations from the past had taken over his mind. First he could hear Madeline saying, "We had to let go, Brian. We couldn't ask her to suffer any longer because we wanted to keep her with us. She suffered enough. It was her choice to go, remember that. She told me that's what she wanted and asked me to understand. Stop feeling like you should have prevented it; you couldn't, none of us could."

But Brian had always known that he could have prevented it, because he should have known the night before she died, when she talked to him far into the night, what she was planning. He had gone over and over everything she said that night, and all he could derive from it was that she wanted Christopher to have a happy life and for Windsong to be his one day. He thought that he had missed something, and yet every word she said was emblazoned on his mind forever, and he tied it into his feelings of guilt. He blamed himself for not having prevented the tragedy. Then his grandfather's voice took over, "Today is here, tomorrow is coming, but yesterday is gone forever." And then the words that the actor like his father had spoken in the play came back to him, and kept echoing in his mind, "There is healing of old wounds, healing and new life, new life, new life for the searchers."

A gentle breeze with the hint of winter tossed the blond curls on Christopher's head as he and Brian stepped out of the truck and walked across the street to the little cemetery. Chris carried the flowers Jennifer had handed him when they were leaving.

As Brian stood with Chris looking down at Joanne's grave, Brian felt the familiar hollowness, and a sense of despair starting to return, when suddenly it was as if Joanne were speaking to him, and her words were swirling around in his head. "Children can't be happy if the parents aren't, and I want Christopher to be happy." The meaning of what she had said took root at last, and the magnitude of what she had done brought tears to his eyes.

Even if he had prevented her from dying he could not have protected Christopher's happiness, because her illness was creating turmoil and destroying all of them. For the first time since Joanne's death he felt less burdened.

He saw Christopher bend down and place the flowers by the plaque that bore her name. Then he stood up and put his hand in Brian's.

"Dad, does Mommy understand about us?"

"Yes, she understands about us; she told me that she wants us to be happy and to have a good life."

"That means she doesn't mind about Jennifer, doesn't it?"

"That means she doesn't mind; it's the way she would want it to be."

They stood together for a time, father and son, in silent tribute to the wife and mother they had both so dearly loved.

"We can go now, Dad," Chris said.

They turned to leave the little cemetery, walking hand in

hand. The prophecy of Cyrus Logan was being fulfilled; the mountains had inspired his descendants. They were becoming strong men.

Epilogue

The Logans still live at Windsong on the bench above the Kicking Horse River and the Trans-Canada Highway, where the wind sings in the trees. And there is a Rocky Mountain bighorn sheep in the pasture with the horses. He has a raised spot on the back of his head between his massive horns where the hair grows straight up, a personal distinction suggesting a battle scar. He tries to herd the horses about, and it is obvious that they detest him. But Christopher and his sister Karri-Lyn love him. They call him Yoho, son of Sam.